CREATE NEW LOVE

*How Men and Women Can Prepare for
a LASTING Relationship*

Anne Stirling Hastings, Ph.D

2012

2

Table of Contents

INTRODUCTION

How are your first dates? Do you try to look your best, present yourself in the best possible light? Do you want him or her to think you are more interesting, intelligent, competent, rich, sexy, attractive, and successful than you feel? Did you read articles about dating? The ones that teach you how to present yourself, ways to get a second date, how to be irresistible?

Wouldn't it be great to start from a very different place when sitting down for that first meeting? Imagine an approach where you would be entirely yourself and expecting that to be valued. Where you would would check out the other person to see if they are capable of relationship intimacy. Where you check to see if he or she wants what *you* want.

I'm going to show you how to begin ***real*** relationships. Skip the magazine articles and go right for the psychological approach to finding the right person and creating a good pairing. And even before you set out to find someone, you can study how relationships really work and what you can learn to enhance your chances for success.

I have been a psychologist for 30 years, helping people after conflicts have already arisen in their relationships. I specialize in sexual healing. Most of the issues began there, but of course couples have other difficulties that impact their sexuality. So off we go to work on those, too, in order for lovemaking to blossom and create intimacy.

The skills I teach people *after* the relationship is in trouble are the very same ones that can allow couples to do better in *creating new love*. So why not teach these skills to people *before* conflicts begin? Why not *prepare* instead of *repair*?

By the time couples make it to my office they have hurt each other deeply. My job is to help them see how they got into the shaming and blaming and silences and pouting and criticism, and how they pulled back from each other. How they tried to pull loose from the tremendous force of the sexual bond, that deep attachment to each other. Or how they tried to cling to it, focusing all their waking minutes on him or her. How they resented sex, or how they felt the absolute need for it. Repairing these relationships is painful and hard. Sometimes impossible.

While exploring online dating over coffee, I watched men try to figure out what to talk about and what to ask. The socially skilled men had an easy time, but what about those good candidates who were shy, or nervous, or intimidated? They are often dismissed because they don't know how to get started.

Most online daters have failed in their past attempts. We know from the divorce rate that half of all of us fail. *Relationship failure is epidemic in our country.* Few people know how to create healthy love relationships. Most people have been through the pain of struggling to make it work, and then the pain of the ending. It is not something to look forward to.

Is there some way to prepare for success?

Yes!

I can help you begin dating in a way that will make the selection process faster and more accurate. Can you imagine discussing with your date the way you go about attaching to someone? You could talk about how to resolve conflicts right away. Perhaps even the real nature of monogamy. Or how sex needs to be respected because it glues people into a couple whether they want it to or not! I would have had a second date with any man who began this way.

PREPARATION COULD BE EASIER

Wouldn't it be even better for *single people* to study healthy interactions with non-lovers first, and then use those new skills with a potential mate?

This book is for those of you who want a love relationship. I will offer you an overview of those areas that create obstacles to relating. I will explain how once you can see areas of difficulty, you can learn how to sidestep them. I will show you how to engage in the *healing of those very causes* of things going wrong. All of this is based on the exciting new research and wisdom of reigning experts who are developing a new understanding of what love is all about.

FALLING IN LOVE

Falling in love is the greatest thing. That wonderful feeling that makes you believe that those smiles won't ever leave your face, and will never leave his or hers. Sitting alone in a coffee shop without feeling alone. And the sex—that wonderful glue that creates a relationship far beyond friendship, that leads people to propose marriage, to bring their lives together, and set out to permanently attach. And then the security of knowing the other person is always there for you.

*That feeling of dependence ironically brings
the freedom of independence*

If problems arise in your life, your partner is there to listen, to sympathize, to help out. Life seems normal. Of course it does. This is how it is supposed to be.

Love brings all those negative emotions, too. This is also programmed into our very DNA. Anger, betrayal, hurt, jealousy, humiliation, and fear. Yes, fear. The fear that she will leave. That he will fall in love with someone else. But there are other fears, too. Even when you know your mate won't leave or be with someone else, you may have a strong sense of needing to know this person, to know what he thinks and feels. A sense of constancy is needed, of predictability, of security, of safety — trust.

When you feel threatened, rage flies up unbidden, doesn't it? And when your partner's rage emerges, you feel devastated and defensive. You want to prove that you didn't do anything wrong.

Here is a vitally important point we will return to in these pages:

All of us will overreact when we are in love.

The same behavior from a friend may be annoying or painful, but from a lover it's devastating. If friends say they don't want to get together because they feel a pull to get things done at home, it's okay. But if a lover says this when you're feeling deep love and desire to be with her, it feels terrible. To have him choose working around the house over being with you? Making love with you? Building on this new relationship? Hurt follows.

4

Here are some typical scenarios. Sound familiar?

- He's a half hour late and doesn't call. She is angry for days.
- She accepts a flirtatious hug from someone else. He calls her names.
- She finds out that he has been seeing an old girlfriend and hiding it from her. She is hurt beyond belief by what he did, and that he hid it.
- She lies about where she has been because she was shopping for a new car that she knows he doesn't want to buy. He senses that she lied. He fears that there is someone else.
- He talks a lot about a new woman at work. She feels threatened and angry.
- He sits in front of the TV while she gets dinner for the 10th day in a row. She simmers. When she asks him to cook, he pouts as if she is asking too much. Resentment builds.
- She wants sex again. He feels pressured and resentful. She feels abandoned, unloved, and unattractive. In other words, devastated.
- She finds him masturbating to porn on the computer. She feels betrayed.

Why is a physical sensation of pain around our hearts so common to all of us? Upset stomachs, great sighs, heat rising out of us? Tears pushing for release, distraction from work, becoming forgetful, and little interest in anything else? Because *love relationships are the most essential connections.*

Why do we have such a hard time with these emotions? Why are they programmed into us? Can they be managed so that our reactions don't harm the relationship? Is it possible to actually heal them out of existence?

The answer is: Yes! Relationship skills can be *learned.* Our divorce-promoting culture has prevented most people from learning this fact early in life. But it is very possible now to discover how to handle those emotions brought on by deep, passionate love. We can learn to resolve conflicts. We can use sexuality in the most relationship enhancing way!

Half of marriages end. We used to think this was caused by fighting over differences in what each wanted—their values, different sexual frequency, kind of sexual interaction, childrearing, family commitments, money. But no. Recent research shows that it's *how these conflicts are handled* that predicts the future of the relationship. When people shame one another, put the other down, call each other names, or retreat into silence, it becomes impossible to find solutions. In fact, John Gottman (*The Seven Principles for Making Marriage Work*) has discovered that he can predict divorce based on thirty minutes of observing a couple's manner of addressing a conflict!

What better place to start than by learning methods that help a relationship instead of ending it?

Couples who are adept at resolving conflicts can handle their differences. Couples who learn how to resolve conflicts *can* learn *to handle their differences!*

THE NATURE OF LOVE ATTACHMENT

The newest relationship research is about the very nature of the attachment. It holds information vital to successful relationships, including how to handle those strong negative emotions.

We have long known that sexual attraction to a loved one creates strong feelings. Songs, poetry, movies, TV, and everything around us reflect that intense feeling. Now researchers have the ability to establish the *changes that go on in the brain* when we fall in love! We now know that this bond between two people is very similar to the one that occurs between a mother and infant! Isn't this amazing? Sexual love is truly central to life. We are wired up to experience it this way.

Once we understand that this connection is vital, we can understand how to protect it, nurture it, and make it safe from harm. *Attached: The New Science of Adult Attachment and How It Can Help You Find and Keep Love,* by Amir Levine, tells us all about attachment styles so we can see how we may be interfering with our very instinctive need to love. Sue Johnson wrote *Hold Me Tight: Seven Conversations for a Lifetime of Lov*e to explain how we can protect that connection.

Both writers, however talk about *undoing* harm. Why not learn about it *before* harm is caused?

PREPARATION OR REPAIR?

Now that you are thinking about a new relationship, you have a chance to learn about what prevented your last attempts from being successful. Perhaps you can remove the obstacles this time. You can look at alternative ways of expressing feelings or needs, and practice replacing unworkable approaches. This is so much easier when not in the heat of conflict!

We will take a look at recent research that reveals how the nature of love relationships is instinctive, what these attachments need in order to flourish, and the skills necessary to make this happen. While looking at changing your styles of conflict resolution, we will also look at all the wonderful ways of supporting the evolution of a truly connected experience, one where you feel safely attached. We will get to understand that safety is far more than believing your partner won't leave, or have sex with someone else. It is a *feeling*, similar to what we needed from our mothers. Only now, *both partners offer it to each other*. It is created through words, touch, eye contact, and honest expression of real feelings and needs.

AND WHAT ABOUT SEX?

It is a myth that the second year of marriage includes a drop in sexual activity. Well, actually, there typically is a drop. The myth is that this is natural and normal, to be expected and accepted. In truth, sex drops off because unresolved conflicts increase. *Couples who are adept at nurturing their relationship and each other continue being sexual.* Johnson differentiates this from sex that is based on infatuation and toys and variety as belonging in the lust category. She says, "Secure bonding and fully satisfying sexuality go hand in hand: they cue off and enhance each other. Emotional connection creates great sex, and great sex creates deeper emotional connection." She goes on to say how secure partners have the safety to fully engage in lovemaking.

Johnson has a term for wonderful love-making that she calls "synchrony sex." This is when emotional openness and responsiveness, tender touch, and erotic exploration all come together. She equates it to the attunement that mothers ideally have for their baby in which she senses the child's inner state and responds to his perceived need. This same non-verbal sensing of each other, now woven with arousal, allows the use of sexuality to enhance the secure bond that sets the loving partner apart from all others.

When couples have difficulty creating a Securely Attached relationship they often fall into what Johnson calls "sealed off sex," or "solace sex." Sealed off sex is for the sake of it, to release sexual tension.

The emotions of love and affection are limited. Solace sex is an attempt to obtain reassurance. It can be a substitute for affection. It is not a safe reassurance as conflicts over frequency and desire can interrupt its purpose as a security blanket.

THE FUNCTION OF SEXUAL GLUE

Using sexual connection and sexual activity to bond together is just as important as learning how to resolve conflicts and understanding our manner of attaching to a loved one. This powerful glue can drive couples apart when not well used, or it can intensify the bond, helping both people feel safe. When a partner complains about not getting enough, or feeling forced to have too much, or refusing to do this or that, sex becomes a performance arena. The glue still operates, but it is filled with rocks and sand that prevent it from achieving its purpose. Talking about it and observing every aspect of it while you are entering a new relationship offers the chance of *enhancing the relationship at its very core*.

FIVE ARENAS OF RELATIONSHIP CREATION

If single people understand the principles of five areas of relating, it can sustain them through that initial process of coming together and carry them through to sustaining a life long relationship.

I. The first arena has to do with styles of *conflict resolution*. When people speak with contempt, criticism, or defensiveness, or react with silence and withdrawal, resentment builds, and the relationship comes closer to ending. With practice, it is possible to change to a positive, effective approach to solving conflicts. Chapter 4 will explain this "make or break" aspect of relationships.

II. Second is the style of *relationship attachment*. Identifying yours, and observing that of a potential partner, can avoid conflicts created by a large difference. For example, if a needy, clingy person mates with an introvert who works a lot, it isn't likely to go well. But if two clingy people, or two introverts, get together, chances are much better that they will have a good fit. Attachment Theory has provided a

8

great deal of information about these styles, how to handle them, and even how to change them. We will address this in Chapter 5.

III. The third area is the use of *sexuality as the glue* to make this the most special of relationships, and to keep it that way. This includes healing sexuality from past influences and from the culture. In Chapter 7 we will address this and one of its simplest but challenging solutions: talking.

IV. We will look at how *shame inhibits comfortable relating* and drives wedges. Shame is the enemy of conflict resolution, leading to irresolvable arguments. Shame makes us put others on a pedestal, or causes us to see ourselves as superior to others, including our partner. Shame reduction increases ease and comfort. Chapter 3 explains how shame interferes with good relating.

V. All of us *project our early relationships* and views of life onto the people around us. The tendency to view people through a specific lens leads to distortion. For example, a man who grew up in loud, angry households might feel attacked when his partner yells from another room. He projects the childhood experience of danger associated with yelling, and it will seem as if he is in danger when she yells, even if she is simply trying to get his attention.

Alternatively, a woman growing up with a mother who punished her with silent withdrawal may be very sensitive to her partner's silence. His quiet moments may seem to be so much more than silence, because as a child it was devastating to her. It seems to be now, too.

Those disciplined with cold stares will respond more strongly to a partner's cold expression.

When these projections enter the relationship, they can be identified. Then you have a good chance of learning how to handle them in relating with others. Even better, they can be healed out of existence.

FURTHER LEARNING

If you want to explore any of these in more depth, the following books elaborate on one of the areas.

•*Hold Me Tight*, by Sue Johnson
•*Attached: the New Science of Adult Attachment and How It Can Help You Find and Keep Love*, by Amir Levine and Rachel Heller.
•*The Seven Principles for Making Marriage Work*, by John Gottman
•*Reclaiming Healthy Sexual Energy: Revised*, by Anne Stirling Hastings
•*Healing Humanity: Life Without Shame*, by Anne Stirling Hastings
•*Getting the Love You Want*, by Harville Hendrix
•*Nonviolent Communication: A Language of Life*, by Marshall Rosenberg

Chapter 1

The Relationship We All Want

Attachment Theory calls the best coupling a "Securely Attached" relationship. It's that very way of life that we are programmed to create, literally in our DNA, and absolutely instinctive. Our hormones and emotions work very hard to obtain it.

We need this understanding so we can make sense of our emotions and how we handle them, as well as our new love's emotions and how she handles them.

I noticed when reading hundreds of profiles on dating sites that most of the men wanted a comfortable, friendly relating to enhance their lives. They made it sound easy and nice. No games, no drama, please. They wanted the ideal for which they were programmed, but didn't know how to get from the first date to the end result. I shook my head, knowing they would wonder why each attempt hadn't worked.

Sadly, most of us were deprived of the good attachment during childhood, which left us unable to automatically form that wonderful experience. But now we can set out to understand what we want, how we prevent it from happening, and how the people we meet prevent it, too. Then we can work toward creating a different kind of relationship – one in which we agree to *learn how to create it together.*

I will describe some of the components of the model that we can work toward. I want to emphasize "work toward," as just learning about it won't automatically make it happen. We need new skills to bring us closer to what is possible. Skills require practice.

NO RELATIONSHIP IS PERFECT

I am going to tell you about the relationship that our instincts want us to have, but, sadly *not a single person gets to have*! I want you to know this so that you don't set out to learn skills that are really challenging, only to find that you can't fully succeed. Really, the American culture interferes. When we have to struggle with the effects of deprivation that all of us had in our very early lives, and the abuses and neglect some of us went through, we fall on a continuum from those who cannot be in relationship at all to those who are doing very well. But even when doing well, no relationship is perfect.

I approach my own learning and healing as an ongoing process. I have no very specific goals, just a desire to constantly improve. I go through the very processes described here to continually eradicate the harmful effects of my childhood and the culture, and increasingly embrace the ongoing ability to love and be loved.

Please do not compare yourself to an ideal. You have no competition! Measure by improvement.

Learn.

Observe.

Practice.

Notice improvement.

Smile!

And then start all over again: learning, observing, practicing, noticing improvement, and smiling!

These healing approaches will be more thoroughly looked into in the second half of the book.

COMMUNICATION

Every self-help book for couples begins with the need for communication. If you can't talk about an issue, it will fester. If it isn't directly addressed, it will be expressed indirectly. This is the source of hurt feelings, misinterpretation, and the passive aggressive expression of anger. Talking doesn't automatically mean that things will go well, but it must start there.

TIME TOGETHER

Couples can avoid conflict by leading separate lives, but they won't have the intimacy that all of us want. Time together will allow the instincts to surface and bring two people into a couple. That's why we have that strong desire to spend a lot of time together in the beginning. We want to combine our lives into one foundation.

INTEREST IN EACH OTHER'S LIVES

Asking about each other's day, really listening to all emotions and thoughts, and supporting the other in various endeavors can create a sense of togetherness. This includes filling each other in on personal histories, both the good and bad; wanting to know about relatives, how each other's families function, the struggles and successes in education and employment.

DEPENDABILITY

Being where you say you will be, and doing what you say you will do are obvious foundations of trust. Suspicion is generated when one person expects the other to be somewhere and repeatedly discovers that they are not. Gentle, ever-present, complete trust can be weakened over even small discrepancies. These can include things like not buying something needed at the store, not cooking when it's your turn, or failing to do your share of the agreed-upon division of labor.

TRUTHFULNESS

Deceit is a powerful obstacle to the intimacy necessary in a Securely Attached relationship. It includes lies, secret keeping, and silences, too. We are all familiar with the dreadful feeling that comes when the other person says he was somewhere, but you know the timing can't be right. You may think you shouldn't suspect, yet you sense that something is off. You may ask if you are right, but you know that if he isn't telling the truth he isn't going to admit that now.

When your partner deceives over and over you will lack trust. Even if you are entirely sure there isn't another person, that distrust eats

14

away at the safety that comes from believing you really know your partner.

Hearing different stories at different times has the same effect. Even more disturbing than conflicting stories is concern over the reason for needing them. Trust erodes.

TRANSPARENCY

The willingness and desire to be completely seen brings your mate a sense of safety and trust. If everything is visible, there is no need to question or suspect. This is a great support to falling deeply in love. There will be no surprises, no threats, no fears.

Even when both people are committed to being transparent, the resulting trust takes time. It is also delayed by varying amounts of hesitation in revealing ourselves. Our entire culture, with its levels of deception and using does not promote a rapid sense of safety. This can be somewhat offset by telling the new date about your hesitation, and that it will take time to trust.

Have you noticed that when someone can say they have a negative reaction to what you said or did, you trust them more? A friend asked me to watch her webinar and evaluate it. I told her all the negatives. She appreciated it, and had not liked that others focused only on positives! She knows that my positive perceptions of her are true because I was willing to give her the negatives.

NO THREATS TO TRUST AND SAFETY

Transparency makes it possible to have differing approaches to relationships without threatening trust. For example, she is feeling loving and close after a wonderful exchange with him. She lovingly invites him to stay at her place the next night. He pauses, then says that he has things to do around his house. She feels rejected and hurt.

If he acts put out she will experience her hurt as valid. While he may be trying to reject what he perceives as her controlling, she may take it to mean he doesn't care.

But if he can step forward and explain, perhaps including his need to pull away from too much closeness, she will be able to trust him. She will know that he isn't leaving her and isn't interested in someone else.

If a couple can talk about it all, they can sort through what is actually threatening to one partner, in contrast to projected emotions from the past. Sue Johnson in *Hold Me Tight* describes ways for couples to have their separate lives and relate with others while reassuring their partner at the same time. Sacrifice and compromise are not healthy. Reassurance usually is.

FIDELITY OR MONOGAMY

Fidelity is usually defined as being sexually faithful by not having sex with someone else. However, flirting, ignoring the partner while talking with another person, becoming too attached to a friend even if not engaging sexually, and acting as if someone else is more attractive, are examples of behavior that can feel threatening.

INTIMACY

Intimacy is defined as knowing and being known by another. It is the natural outcome of honesty, fidelity, interest, transparency, and communication. You will know each other so well that your relationship can feel like a dance where you naturally and easily alternate leading and following. It is inherent in Secure Attachment.

ARE YOU COMMITTED?

This brings us to a central question. Are you interested in working toward the most Securely Attached relationship? If you are, you will have your work cut out for you. You will need to discover your attachment style, your attachment behaviors, your relationship fears, your non-human attachment replacements, and be willing to face up to any discomfort as you and your love work toward secure attachment. You will need to face your feelings of shame in order to let them go, and you will want to discover the true purpose of sexuality. And you will need to accept the speed at which you can accomplish difficult tasks.

If this is what you desire, this book will lay out the path to move in that direction.

Chapter 2

Then the Emotions Come!

Remember those emotions I talked about in the Introduction? Well, here they come! Those intense, seemingly exaggerated feelings of anxiety, jealousy, and anger. If only he or she would look just at you, focus on you, love you, then everything would be wonderful.

New research on the brain has helped affirm the power of the romantic connection. We are actually wired up to connect with a partner in the same physiological manner as infants are with mothers. The changes in the brain and in our hormones are identical in many ways.

Its clear that babies and mothers have intense emotions regarding each other. Remember when you were gone for the day how you couldn't get the little one out of your mind? And we were the adults. The baby's experience of being left is known to everyone. Sobbing and distress indicate the level of fear and hurt that is felt over the experience of being abandoned. To a baby it is life and death because its brain isn't sufficiently mature to understand that Mom will return.

EMOTIONS FROM THE PAST ARE ADDED ON

Now that we understand the similarity between the physiology of babies and lovers, we can appreciate the intensity of emotion that accompanies the sexually glued relationship. And not only do we experience the natural love-related emotions, but we add on those that are projected from childhood. The three year old who was in the hospital for days may very well at age 30 fear that a lover will leave her alone with strangers. And the person sexually abused may believe that her partner will violate her this way, too.

It is all very complex. We need information in order to make sense of what goes on between us, and the skills to handle it. One guideline is to look at our strong emotions as a combination of those from the past and those legitimate in the present. Perhaps only 10% is from the present, leaving 90% projected from childhood or earlier life.

PROTECTING EACH OTHER

When we can appreciate our instinctive wiring, we are more likely to grasp that when our lover is having strong feelings, it isn't about what we did. This opens us to more compassion and acceptance. And then *we can repair even if we did nothing wrong.*

Now is the time to employ communication, honesty, and transparency in order to flow more easily through these unavoidable reactions when falling for someone. You don't even have to fall very hard in the beginning to trigger some of them.

If you are postponing the beginning of a relationship, this is a good thing. It will allow you to practice relationships skills with people you are not in love with. The emotional intensity can be avoided for the time being, which usually allows the mind to see more clearly!

The information below is written for those beginning new relationships and for those who are waiting. If not in a relationship, you can use your imagination while you practice the skills.

CREATING SECURITY

Chapter One took a look at defining a Securely Attached relationship. Now we can look at how we can protect each other from feeling threatened.

The fear that he or she will end the relationship, or take a sexual interest in someone else, are universally seen as valid. Most everyone is concerned with such things. But even if you don't have these fears, you can still expect to have discomfort. These fragile, new connections are so vital to our sense of a good life, of community, and of purpose, that countless fears pop up that seem to make no sense.

If she flirts, why is that painful? Even if you know there is no real threat of loss, sexual attention directed elsewhere *feels threatening.* The difference between *seeming* threatening, and actually *being* threatening is only a matter of degree. If we understand this, we can have compassion for ourselves and our partner when irrational emotions surface. We can also understand that our new partner will have strong emotions that we are not causing.

Simple examples of actions that seem threatening are: not calling each day; sounding distracted or uninterested; being preoccupied with something else without talking about it; staying on the phone too long when together; frequently canceling plans, and so on.

There is nothing wrong with any of those behaviors. All are within the normal realm of life. But when in a new relationship, we need to understand that they will trigger feelings of hurt or fear, and we have a chance to do something about it. *Telling* your love what is going on, why you can't call, what work is requiring, or that you just need time alone can alleviate much distress. When you are the one with the emotions, you can acknowledge that you are having discomfort from being in love. You can ask questions in order to learn the truth as soon as possible.

HOW TO REPAIR

If you understand why your love is having strong emotions, even if you have done nothing harmful, you are in a position to *repair the hurts anyway*. You can remember that if you feel guilt or shame, and become defensive, it isn't necessary! He is just having those normal love relationship feelings! How wonderful if you are able to put them to rest, to reassure, to hold hands, to declare your love. What if you can see that you could easily make changes that would help your lover feel better? Wouldn't it be wonderful to do so?

Even when you see that you can't make changes because it wouldn't be the right thing to do, you can demonstrate compassion for your partner's emotions.

For example, you have been struggling to understand something needed at work, and finally, it becomes clear. You are pulled to work on it even though it is a Saturday morning when you and your love were going to hang out casually in bed and over coffee. If you leap out of bed, how will he feel? But you know you can't be present to the loving because you have found the solution to your problem at work. What you can do is to hug him, and explain what you have figured out. You can tell him how sorry you are that you are not in the mood for the laid-back plans the two of you had. And then you can get to work.

Repair begins with understanding that *your partner is having strong emotions caused by entering a Securely Attached relationship*. If you can listen attentively, and have empathy and compassion, she will begin to feel better. If she is allowed to have anger and hurt, she can discharge them and then be ready to talk about what's next. Your job is to listen and *try* to not feel defensive. You may find that you want to lash out, or say it's her fault, or tell her what she should do so you don't feel hurt. Defensiveness is difficult to interrupt. It takes ongoing practice.

Then you can talk about the need for change, if any. She may say, "I see that you need me to call if I'm going to be more than 15 minutes late. I'll do that."

He might say, "Even though I have no attraction to the woman I have lunch with at work, I see that it is upsetting to you, so I won't do it anymore. I get that if you had lunch with a man regularly I wouldn't like it either. I didn't think about it because there really is nothing going on."

Let's say that for some reason he had to have lunch with the woman because of job requirements. Perhaps she represented a vendor of his company. He could talk with his lover about what might be acceptable to her. He could think about this by wondering what would be okay for him if the tables were turned. He might come up with the idea of ordering lunch and having it delivered to them in the conference room. This would ensure a more formal approach to business while still allowing a lunch-time meeting. He might tell his lover that if she were having a business lunch with a man, this would feel okay to him, so he hoped it was for her. *She will be reassured that he thought this through, took her feelings seriously, and clearly wanted both of them to protect the relationship.*

WHEN HURT IS TRIGGERED

A man in a new relationship might have said, "When I turn down your invitation to stay over because I want to get things on my long list done, I see that this felt hurtful when you were feeling so open and loving. Next time I'll try to tell you what's going on, what I need to do, and how strong the pull between you and the list is. Now that we're talking about it, I see why you would feel hurt when this is just a list of things, and you wanted to share love. I was an idiot! I turned you down for a stupid list!"

Or he might have told her that after spending so much loving time with her, he felt as if his life were on hold. That he needed to go back to the ordinary things he usually did around his house and yard, activities with friends. He could explain that their new relationship was disconcerting, and it would feel good to go back to "normal" for a little while. "But I can call you to say goodnight," he might add. *It is possible for him to meet his needs, and at the same time, protect the relationship.*

WHEN FEAR IS TRIGGERED

My friends Susan and Bob were in a relationship for a few months when both of them accidentally triggered fear in the other. Bob put up pictures of himself and Susan on Facebook. But in thinking it over, he realized that he didn't want to share those personal items with some of the people looking at his Wall, so he took them down. When Susan went on his page, she was really hurt. Why had he hidden pictures of her? She made up that he was ashamed of their relationship, ashamed of her, and didn't want people to know about them. She made it up!

So then Susan checked the box on her page saying she was in relationship, and then the box, "It's complicated." When Bob saw this he believed that she wasn't really committed to him after all.

In her usual distancing approach to conflict, Susan thought it was over. She would have to leave someone who felt this way. She fumed. All of this emotion was based on what she had made up about his dedication to their relationship!

Bob was more forthright. He was unwilling to sit around in apprehension at his office all day. He drove to her house, walked in, and said "We need to talk."

These are the kind of emotions that appear in therapists' offices as issues to be addressed. Why does he do this, why did she do that? What's wrong with the other person for hurting me?

Instead, *let's assume that strong emotions from misinterpretations are normal!* Then we can take a different approach.

Bob explained that he wanted to keep the pictures private, and had no idea this would frighten her. He would put them back up. He put his arms around her and told her that he was proud to be with her, and wanted the whole world to know. He didn't want his ex-wife and her relatives peering into his new life, but he would handle that.

Once she could understand, Susan felt loved and reassured. Of course he didn't want their loving faces criticized. Her heart warmed.

Earlier, when Bob first arrived at her door, Susan was shocked by how he had looked. She thought someone had died. She reached out to him, asking what it was. When he told her, she was equally shocked! What a strong reaction for something so small! But it wasn't small. These are *normal, natural emotions that most people experience.*

Susan explained that she checked "complicated" because she had just seen the removed pictures, and was in the midst of strong feelings. She had removed the check mark two minutes later. Bob had looked at her Wall during those two minutes.

If both of them carried resentment about what the other had done, they would be off to therapy sessions a year or five down the line. But neither was willing to sweep it under the carpet. Both knew that communication was essential.

As they held onto each others hands, both angrily shook their heads, discharging the despairing emotions. He said, "I hated that you did that! I was so afraid that you weren't really with me, and I just couldn't stand it!"

Because she knew that these feelings are natural to a love relationship, she could actually feel good that he had such a strong reaction. She surprised him by smiling! She knew that because *he had such strong feelings of love, he would have equally strong feelings of fear.*

One night they were at a meeting, and Susan sat next to a man she had known for years. Bob was on her other side. When she touched the man as a hello, he responded flirtatiously, his tone implying that she was expressing sexual interest in him. She didn't realize this, but Bob did. He leaned forward, looked at the man, and told him to stop. He did.

When back in their car, Bob told Susan that he needed to talk right then about his feelings because he didn't want them to *fester.* He knew he would make up horrible scenarios if he let things go. Susan was curious, wanting to know what was upsetting him. He told her that he was jealous, and it felt terrible to think of her relating with sexual energy with anyone else. He wanted her all for himself.

Susan told me that a year before she would have been angry about being accused. She hadn't flirted. She didn't invite her friend's interest. She didn't deserve to have her man treat her as if she did!

But after learning that these intense feelings are normal, Susan again felt loved! If he weren't capable of jealousy, he wouldn't be so deeply in love with her. Once her shame about being seen as someone who causes a lover harm had dropped, she could see the truth. He loved her. He didn't like any infidelity, conscious or not, big or small.

As they entered the tenth month of their relationship. Susan called me in despair one morning, believing that she should wait for Bob's divorce to be final before continuing to be in relationship with him.

What had he done? I waited to hear.

It turns out he had done absolutely nothing threatening! He was waiting for the divorce to be final. His ex was to open her own checking account and leave him the joint one. But she hadn't done it. And Bob hadn't followed through by removing his automatic payments from that account so that he could close it and open one for himself. He hadn't gotten around to it. The ex didn't take money from it, so no problem.

Who is right and who is wrong here? The answer is, *no one.*

Bob isn't violating Susan by not following through. He isn't attached to his ex, the account doesn't feel joint even while her name is still on it. He did nothing wrong!

Susan wants to be the center of his life and the most important person to him. The love emotions make her feel betrayed when Bob does certain things. This is built into her attachment wiring. There is no way out of it.

Both are right. *He didn't hurt her. She feels hurt.*

The solution is for her to tell him that she is hurt, and would he please end that connection with another woman. And when he understands, he will want to do that for her. Not because he did something wrong, but because he has learned that this is hurtful to her— even while he has not hurt her!

RELATIONSHIP SYSTEMS

In the above examples, the relationship system between Susan and Bob became activated. We use the term, "relationship system" to address the way couples relate that aren't based on their real relationship. Each employs projected reactions from childhood along with triggers from the partner. Identifying those systems can help us remain conscious of our irrational emotions and behaviors and then stop them sooner rather than later.

This couple's relationship system goes something like this: Susan responds to hurt with the desire to leave and end the relationship.

She tells him that she doesn't think she can continue with him. All of this is in response to pictures taken down from Facebook.

Bob feels terrible when he hurts someone, especially his love. So he feels compelled to prove that he hasn't hurt her, or that she shouldn't feel hurt. Then he becomes defensive when "accused." Of course he is feeling accused when she says she can't stay in the relationship.

Instead of being able to see her hurt, knowing he didn't cause it, he wants to attack back, defend, feel terrible about himself, and push her away. Then she feels alone, and even more like getting out, or getting him out. And he feels even more hurtful and defensive. *A circular argument is underway!* In other words, a series of mistaken assumptions and reactions is underway.

It has taken time for them to understand that their emotions are normal reactions to falling in love. Once they can do that, they will know how to alleviate them.

MORE EXAMPLES

•Sharon's relationship of almost a year had gone really well. Her new love called her every night, even while he led a busy life and could only see her once or twice a week. But she felt loved, anyway. He was attentive, transparently revealed his activities, and showed his interest.

Then he didn't call one day. Or the next. Sharon's mind created the belief that it was from lack of interest, his readiness to move on, and his inability to tell her that. She was hurt. Actually, devastated. She told me that she believed all of this to be true, and she had to grieve out the relationship. I had no way of knowing the truth, either.

But he did call the next day. Being incredibly busy at work was compounded by getting sick, and he just wasn't up to talking. He sounded sincere. She didn't tell him that she had been frightened.

Handling this kind of experience this way is typical in our culture. It is based on "logical" approaches to relationships. They go like this: she shouldn't have worried; she should have called him; she shouldn't question him without concrete evidence.

But now we know that this isn't true! *The relationship needs to be supported by consistency and communication* or any one of us will respond the way Sharon did! And then doubt ourselves—or get friends to support us in our anger about being treated like that. Right?

Sharon and her lover could have supported the relationship with an agreement to communicate everything. If Sharon's man knows that she will naturally respond this way to his lack of calling, he can tell her that he can't talk! A one-minute conversation would reassure her, and he would still have his boundaries. Or Sharon could have called him, explain that she was triggered into fear because of her love for him and their relationship. She could have learned the truth instead of making it up. If they both understand that *strong emotions emerge from falling in love, and they must be attended to*, then they could both be happy with either of these solutions.

•When Lisa walked into a bar and saw her husband sitting next to a woman who was touching him as if she were coming on to him, Lisa was upset. Her husband wasn't responding, but Lisa was distressed anyway. Why wasn't he telling the woman that he wasn't available, and to stop coming on to him?

Lisa and her husband didn't understand the principles of Securely Attached relationships, so they spent the evening fighting. He defended himself by saying that he wasn't interested and had done nothing to provoke the woman's behaviors. Lisa criticized him for even letting the woman do what she did.

If her husband understood why Lisa reacted, he could have smiled, put his arms around her, and said, "I'm so glad you didn't like that! I know you really want me all to yourself."

Lisa could ask him to not let women do that. He would agree because he would see that this behavior so common in bars was hurtful to his wife. It was hurtful to the relationship. He would look forward to the next time he could turn a flirting woman away in the service of his marriage.

•Alan and his fiancée were at a college dance when a friend of hers walked up wearing a low-cut dress and broadcasting sexual energy. Alan said, "Hi, Sexy." His fiancée slapped him. He was stunned. Both were silent for the rest of the evening, barely able to be in each other's presence. It was never discussed, and remained one event in a very long list of grievances that led to divorce years later. They didn't know that their sexual issues came from that list, resulting in her lack of interest in him. Years into their marriage she gave up sex as relationship glue, and then no longer reacted when he flirted with or sexualized women. *Without strong love, the intense emotions are no longer provoked.* Divorce occurs when none of this is understood.

She might have turned to him and said something like, "It felt like you were being unfaithful. It feels horrible when you call someone else sexy. I want all of your sexual energy with me, with us. That's the only way we can remain in love."

If Alan were truly in love and understood Secure Attachment, he might have realized that he had exhibited a hurtful infidelity by making that comment. He would have apologized and listened to his lover as she cried out her hurt. Then he would have told her that he loved only her, really loved being sexual with her, and would stop responding to women who wanted his attention. He thought that "real men" were supposed to react to sexy women. After thinking about it, he might have suggested what he could have said instead. Or he could have just turned his back and smiled down at his fiancée.

•"I thought you were going to call." This is a classic statement. When she says this, he feels pressured and resentful. Then he doesn't want to call the next day either. Her distress increases. When couples talk every day, they both feel reassured. They are intact. But if it becomes a conflict area, they will need to talk about it. Instead of the usual question, she could tell him that it made her uncomfortable to wait for his call and then realize it wasn't coming. She was frightened that he was pulling away, that he didn't care.

She could say, "When you don't call, it makes me feel separate from you, not really a couple. I get scared and wonder about us, even though you say we are a couple. Can we talk about what to do about that?"

If he understands the power of love to evoke emotion, he will want to do what he can to avoid that pain. He may explain that he only has ten minutes most evenings when he is working, but he will call her. And he will want to understand that it's her love that brings the emotion. She isn't controlling just for the sake of it.

If she cries or is angry, he can smile! How nice to be so loved!

•Partial answers to questions will provoke fear, too. If a friend avoided answering your question you might wonder why, but if your lover does, fear or anger can arise. What is she hiding? Why can't he answer? You may be afraid that if you ask about it, she will get mad at you for not trusting her.

But if she *understands the emotions triggered by love*, she will want to fill you in. She will elect transparency over causing you discomfort.

•Rick had a long-standing friendship with an old lover, and they had been casually sexual a few months before he met Nancy. He neglected to tell Nancy that he still went out to dinner and emailed extensively. When she inadvertently found out, she was very upset and considered ending the relationship. Rick became more open, but didn't acknowledge that Nancy had a right, as his lover, to be upset. When she said that she couldn't tolerate it if he spent any more time with the old lover, he refused to cooperate. She couldn't fully trust him even though she believed he wasn't going to have sex with anyone else.

If Rick understood relationship emotions, and the need to protect each other, he would have realized how hurtful his behavior had been, apologize, and assure her that he wouldn't relate with any old lover. He would see that in order to develop her trust in him, he had to step forward and demonstrate an appreciation of relationship needs.

Rick felt shame over his need to separate his life into compartments, and deceive others in order to accomplish that. This prevented him from understanding what he had done, what his lover needed to feel, and how to repair. He deeply did not want to hurt anyone, especially her. But his shame was so strong that when he did hurt others, he wanted to deny it. He rationalized it away. He tried to get his lover to avoid feeling strongly. In fact, he could not see why he shouldn't relate with the old lover, and resented his lover for "making" him stop.

Research has demonstrated that defensiveness in conflict resolution predicts divorce. Rick was unable to let it go and repair the damage. Was divorce coming?

•Eddie's new partner wore clothing that revealed much of her breasts and other body parts. While he liked this when they met, once she became his woman, he found it distressing to think that other men lusted after her. In time she came to understand that he saw her breasts as important in their making love, and that they should not be presented as sexual to others. When she could relinquish the belief that he was trying to control and own her, she could understand his legitimate distress. She could smile, too, and change her clothing.

HOPE THAT IT WILL CHANGE

Chapter 8 addresses the common practice of trying to get the other person to change. The emotion that is experienced is the one of hope. Hope is forward reaching, looking into the future, imagining something that isn't true in the present, and wanting something that doesn't exist.

This emotion can be useful, of course. To hope that you will get a job, or that someone you care for will get well is fruitful and encourages a positive approach to life. But when hope is misplaced, it will distract you from reality, or it can alter your perception of reality. It actually interferes with life because energy is directed where it will do no good. The addiction recovery community calls it *hope addiction* when it is an artificial emotion used to change one's experience even if it truly cannot change your life. It has also been called *addiction to potential*: when you see the partner's potential, and believe that you can get him or her to develop it.

Asking the person to change, and using new conflict resolution skills in the process, is healthy and good for the relationship. But when it fails, you have a choice between accepting the person as is or leaving. That said, women tend to hang on, believing the impossible is possible. And, after all, if you see that he has great potential, wouldn't you want to stay around and make sure he develops it? So what if he has an affair twice a year, confesses, and promises never to do it again – you just know that he wants to be faithful. Or what if he gambles away your money, putting you in danger of not being able to pay the bills. Do you brush it aside, responding to his desperation with forgiveness and hope for change – even when you have gone through the same thing many times?

If you depend on useless hope, it will help to identify it so that you can choose better, and accept better.

SHAME

*Shame is an obstacle to understanding
our partner's strong emotions regarding
any hint of danger to the relationship.*

If we believe that we are to blame, and feel badly about ourselves for it, then we are likely to become defensive. Notice in the chapter on conflict resolution that chronic defensiveness is one of four predictors of divorce.

I have included information on shame because it is so present in all our lives and in the culture around us, that it is an essential component of understanding a good relationship. The next chapter will offer information about how to recognize shame, and how you avoid feeling it. We all feel it when accused. Relationship emotions will trigger it. And we can prevent ourselves from reacting to it by

understanding these emotions and what is needed to protect the relationship.

Chapter 3

Relationship Shame

In my book, *Healing Humanity: Life Without Shame*, I describe how shame is caused by our culture, and how it prevents world peace. And of course, how it interferes with relationship peace.

WHAT IS SHAME?

First let's define it. Shame extends from simple embarrassment all the way to dreadful badness. It can be a fleeting reaction, or a steady state of negative self-regard. It can take the form of self-hate that comes from seeing that we have done something harmful or wrong – or even thinking we have. You know that feeling that washes over your body and you wish you were anywhere else or feeling anything else?

We can take a look at ongoing forms of shame. Some of these are self-hate, defensiveness about what another person is saying, feeling incompetent when not, hating someone for thinking badly of you, and gossiping to defend your position.

Here is the definition of shame from *Healing Humanity: Life Without Shame.*

> *"Most simply, shame is a terribly unpleasant emotion. Healthy shame is a gentle alert that tells us we would be happier if we shifted gears. Toxic shame, a term offered by John Bradshaw in his best seller,* Healing the Shame That Binds You *(1988), is that dreadful sense of badness. It can include feeling pointless and hopeless, deadened, with no reason to go on. It is the greatest enemy of living a rich, communal life.*

> *"Shame can be experienced in many ways, including anxiety, depression, loneliness, yearning for love and contact, wanting*

32

evidence of success, and fear of being seen. It can be a heaviness that separates one from other people, and from oneself. Apathy, lack of interest and lack of pleasure are signs that shame is dominating."

Now here's an important fact that many people don't know or understand, but it is pivotal in forming healthy relationships:

*Shame is provoked by
being in a love relationship!*

When those intense feelings I described in the last chapter aren't understood, they tend to incite even more shame. When another person acts as if we have hurt them, whether we have or not, we very likely will feel some shame. In the last chapter I explained how our emotions are to be expected, and how we have not caused most of them. I was attempting to reduce your shame through helping you understand this.

When your partner reacts defensively to your emotions, you may feel shame from that, too. This is because when someone is defensive, they are defending against their shame by blaming you. Being defensive implies that you have done something to cause it, that you are the harmful one.

You may find yourself feeling that dreadful emotion of shame first for having the strong emotions, and second, for the reaction of your partner. This shame breeds circular arguments where each person is *defending against feeling shame by shaming*, and then each has to defend harder against the additional shame. And around and around.

Here's an example:

"You should have called!"
"Stop nagging me."
"I don't nag, you always say I nag when all I'm doing is bringing up what you did."
"You criticize me over every little thing. When are you going to stop?"
"No I don't, you're always so mean to me it makes me cry."
This can go on for hours without either remembering that it started with a response to not receiving a call.

*Relationship shame is intense because
all emotions within the relationship are intense!*

Shaming each other and feeling shame tend to be more pronounced in the love relationship than anywhere else. The person you shame the most is the person you love the most!

FEELING LOVED REDUCES SHAME – FOR A WHILE

First you fall in love and have that wonderful sensation of being completely accepted and adored. At last *your shame drops away* as you see yourself mirrored back in her face. You feel stronger, things that normally bother you don't. This is how you are supposed to feel! Love is the answer!

UNTIL THE SHAMING BEGINS

She starts having difficulty with something you said. Or did. Or wanted. She frowns. Perhaps she cries. You feel terrible for hurting her, but you don't understand how you hurt her! You haven't yet read Chapter 2 about those intense emotions that only come in love relationships.

First you get defensive. You want to prove that you didn't do it. Or if you did, that it shouldn't have hurt. Or if it did hurt, that it's her fault that she felt hurt. Or you accept the blame, apologize, and try to make it right. But the shame has lodged in you. It has begun.

You pull back a little. You don't want that feeling to come up again. You are more careful. But being more careful means you have to watch and observe. And then the attachment weakens.

The sexual glue that brought you together so powerfully also weakens. You may want less sex. Or you are likely to base it more on need than love. It becomes a pleasurable activity instead of bringing that sense of fully opening to each other, merging lives and selves, and marrying in your hearts.

Then even this pulling back can be shamed. She complains that you don't love her as much any-more. Something is wrong with you. If you don't know that the emotion of shame is preventing full loving, you will feel more shame. You may try to find solutions. Act this way, make love that way. But

if you can't look at the shame that is now
triggered within the love relationship,
you can't find solutions.

HEALING SHAME

Those who want the most Securely Attached, loving relating can benefit by taking a look at this emotion that we all carry pretty much from birth. Please read *Healing Humanity* to understand how shaming is going on all around us, all the time. I spent days with my computer in various coffee shops, writing and listening. Parents speak shamingly to children when telling them where to sit, what not to touch, how loudly to speak. It was unusual to hear a mother set limits and give instruction without that added tone of impatience, of annoyance at having to say this just one more time.

I overheard countless people gossiping about others. Two or three women acted as if they were having an intimate conversation as they put others down. They enjoyed it. They felt connected to each other. But in fact, they were just relieving the *feeling* of shame. They were not actually connecting intimately.

OBSERVING SHAMING

The first task is observing people shaming others, and those who are trying to relieve their experience of shame. I wrote a chapter called, "Ordinary, Everyday Shame" to help people see what is right in front of us. We take it for granted because we have been exposed to it our whole lives. It seems normal. Meeting with others who are also studying shame speeds up this process because a new sub-culture forms, a sub-culture that *sees shaming*. This can counter living in a culture that doesn't see.

LOOKING AT HOW YOU SHAME OTHERS

If you explore this behavior with a group of people who are examining what they themselves do, it can provoke less shame. Since you know that they shame, too, and actually everyone shames others, your shame may be modulated. Perhaps you won't even feel any!

Take a look at how you shamed your partners. Did you push them away by commenting on how they ordered food? How they interacted with a server? How they drove? Did you ask why she wore that outfit? Or when he last had his hair cut? Or comment twice on the lack of salt in the food? How she didn't listen well?

These very subjects can be addressed without shaming. When you notice that you are asking questions in a shaming manner, you could ask yourself how you really feel. Are you curious? Puzzled? Concerned? Angry? Critical? Notice how you feel. Think about what it would feel like if someone talked to you in the same tone.

LOVE BRINGS
SHAMING, DEFENSIVENESS, AND DISTANCING!

When you are the recipient of those emotions addressed in the last two chapters, you are likely to feel shame. If we don't understand why our partner will have strong emotions, *our* shame will be triggered.

> *If we understand that it is normal to feel angry and jealous,*
> *and that this comes from intense love,*
> *then perhaps we won't feel shame!*

Instead we can feel loved!

When shame emerges, we need to *talk about it*. It is just one more natural experience that comes with loving. It's too bad that we are set up to feel it. *Shame will be provoked!* Better to know this and accept it. Then you can have in place what to do about it.

FIRST, NAME THE SHAME EMOTIONS.

•I feel awful. I have that hot sensation flowing up my chest. I want to cry. I really don't want to hurt you. I don't want to hurt anyone.

•When I saw you looking at that other woman, I felt horrible. I think you don't love me. Then I wonder what that means about me. Am I not attractive to you?

•When you ignore me and act as if I have done something inexcusable, I am devastated. I think it must be all over for us, and I wonder what is wrong with me.

SECOND, NAME HOW YOU TYPICALLY MANAGE YOUR SHAME.

•I want to tell you that it's not my fault.

•I want to believe that if you hadn't done that, I wouldn't have done this.

•I want to protest and ask why you can't just say what you feel without crying or yelling.

•Please don't ignore me. If you have something that we need to process, let's do it. Let's get help with it.

THIRD, LAUGH TOGETHER!

Once you can see that strong emotions are normal, and feeling shame for being "caught" is normal, too, then you have the opportunity to see all of this for what it is. You can hold hands, and smile at each other. Perhaps say some key phrases to remind yourselves. For example,

"Feelings. Shame. Love."

"If I love you I'm going to hate you, too!"

"If you love me you're going to hate me, too."

Healing Humanity: Life Without Shame (available at Amazon.com) offers exercises to do with others in order to reduce the shame we all carry. While feeling that dreadful emotion isn't pleasant, the process of *working together with others* who are healing theirs, too, can be energizing, fun, and help you feel really good about yourself!

Mindful meditation is a practice in which you focus entirely on yourself, breathe deeply, check out each body part, and become aware of what you are feeling. While this kind of inward attention is automatic for many of us who have been involved in emotional healing, the connection with the term *"mindful"* is useful because a great deal has been written on the subject. A practice with a very long history, it has only recently been introduced to therapists as a practice used in sessions, and to teach their clients. The functional MRI (fMRI) has allowed study of the positive changes in the brain following training in Mindfulness as a tool to reduce stress.

Focus entirely on yourself, breathe consciously,
check out each body part, and
become aware of what you are feeling.

Using this technique during conversation with a partner allows a break in tension, and increases the ability to observe what is going on. This is particularly valuable during resolution of conflicts.

Chapter 4

Conflict Resolution

At least some of the time we all use harmful shaming approaches to resolving conflicts. They are reinforced by our culture. They become habit. First we need to see what we do, and then relieve ourselves of the shame that accompanies this realization. If we have to defend ourselves against knowing how we cause harm, we will have difficulty observing ourselves and being open to change. So take a breath! *It's not your fault that you have these habits.*

STYLES OF CONFLICT RESOLUTION

John Gottman, a foremost relationship researcher, discovered that if couples depended on one or more of four styles of conflict resolution, their relationships had little chance of success. They were doomed by negativity. These four styles are described in his book, *The Seven Principles for Making Marriage Work,* which offers exercises to help couples change their approach to conflict.

What if you start exploring your styles of relating *before* entering a relationship? What if you could practice changing that style with strangers? Or take a look with a new person you were dating, instead of with a partner you might have repeatedly hurt? Or who had hurt you?

Now that we know the real nature of love relationships, and that this attachment resembles the intensity of that between a mother and baby, it becomes clear why conflicts and strong reactions to them are to be expected. And why they need special attention in order to help a relationship ease along as well as possible.

FOUR HARMFUL STYLES

The first style is <u>criticism</u>. Instead of saying, "I don't like it when you don't follow through on your commitments," you say something like, "You are such a lazy, thoughtless person, so inconsiderate of me and my feelings!"

The second is <u>contempt</u>. This is expressed with words, tones and facial expression. Gottman's studies discovered that couples who express contempt get more colds, flu, etc. Yikes! More good reasons for changing styles of conflict resolution.

The third is <u>defensiveness</u>. When attacked, people will instinctively defend in order to avoid feeling shamed. But defensiveness is actually an attack, too, which then leads to circular arguments. The attack goes back and forth.

The fourth destructive style is <u>stonewalling</u>. Gottman describes this as looking like an impassive stone wall. The partner using this style tunes out, stops engaging, doesn't talk, and pulls into himself or herself.

Are you noticing which ones you have used in relationships? Which ones your partners have used?

Here's a problem. All of these methods are accepted in our culture! *Friends support our criticism of our mates*. We agree that he or she is stupid, mean, or lazy, as if naming the problem will somehow make it different.

PROJECTIONS

The style of the attempt to handle differences is complicated by the fact that *all of us project our relationship histories onto our partner*.

•For example, the man who grew up in a family in which everyone led their own independent lives came to believe that couples don't relate closely. So he may be distressed when his lover wants to spend a lot of time with him. He may see her as clingy and needy instead of just different from him. This will interfere with their seeing this as just one component of *a conflict that can be resolved*.

•If she was unloved in childhood while being told that she was loved, she may project this onto her lover, and assume that he doesn't care when he actually does. This can create conflicts and arguments unless her history is understood and taken into account. Harville Hendrix explains this in *Getting the Love You Want*. Individual or couple therapy may be needed to help map out these projections so the couple can avoid the consequences of believing things that aren't true.

•If he was expected to do yard work and housework that isn't appropriate for a child and that interfered with his normal social development, he may over-react when his lover points out that he doesn't do any yard or housework. If he understands that his emotions are over-reactions, he has a starting place from which to resolve the impending conflict. When partners are able to describe their typical projections, they can watch for them and take them into account.

Chapter 8, "When the Present Looks Like the Past, But Isn't," addresses how we project our histories. It offers ways to prevent our past from hurting our current relating, as well as how to heal these wounds into nonexistence.

PREPARATION INSTEAD OF REPAIR

The books I recommend have many examples of conflict resolution methods, but of course the couples they discuss have to go back and *undo* the hurt they have caused.

Instead, you can practice using loving, communicative, honest, open and *connecting* ways of addressing conflict. It is so much more empowering and self-caring to set out to *develop a new skill* than it is to have to go back and repair hurts you have caused, isn't it? And hurts that you have suffered? Can you imagine getting to be with others who are developing these skills, too, so you can join together to learn how to create healthy relationships? Conflicts can become arenas for couples to work on with each other instead of tearing the relationship apart.

We will look at these styles in more detail, and look at how to change them. Understanding how shame plays throughout each harmful option will assist in the healing of shame, and allow a transition to useful ways of resolving conflict.

Chapter 5

Attachment Style of Relating

The powerful new approach to parenting and coupling called Attachment Theory began in the 50's with the study of children and parents. It has vastly changed the relating between parents and newborns in hospitals. The study of adult relationships began in the last 20 years, and is quickly making its way into psychotherapy training and practice. Johnson, in *Hold Me Tight,* reviews some of the research that I will summarize here. *Attached,* by Amir Levine, describes the attachment styles and how to recognize them.

Research shows us that *the very instinctive nature of love relationships varies from what the culture idealizes.* We can discover this new understanding for ourselves and develop skills to move toward it!

Johnson tells us how the mental health field has supported the idea that healthy relationships are made up of two independent people who couple. Words such as codependent, symbiotic, undifferentiated and fused have been used to describe people who have difficulty being self-sufficient.

New studies reveal that *when people have "effective dependency" they become more self-sufficient and independent!* The father of Attachment Theory, John Bowlby, talked about how *being able to turn to others for emotional support from "the cradle to the grave" is a sign and source of strength.*

BENEFITS OF SECURELY ATTACHED RELATIONSHIPS

Studies of Secure relationships yield five main ways that they benefit people:

44

1. Seeking Support

When we feel generally secure – comfortable with closeness and confident about our loved ones – we are better at seeking support. When we don't count on others we withdraw into ourselves.

2. Handling inevitable hurts

When feeling securely attached to our partners, we find it easier to handle hurts and are less likely to employ aggressive hostility when we get mad at them.

3. Understanding ourselves better and liking ourselves more

The secure base created with a loved one allows us to be more curious and open to new information. We can be curious when we feel safe. We become rigid when we are vigilant to threats.

4. The more we can reach out to our partners the more separate and independent we can be!

Isn't this amazing? It is a seeming paradox. *As we become dependent where it is natural and appropriate, we become able to be independent in our lives and choices and interactions with others.* What a great reason to learn how to develop a Securely Attached relationship!

5. Physical health and a longer life

While this isn't in the emotional arena, it is powerful information. People in conflicted, stressful relationships become ill more frequently and die earlier. Those in loving, supportive, dependent relationships live longer!

This research shows us that the usual reasons for finding a partner are only the beginning. Some want to marry and create a family, some want to avoid loneliness, others want to experience love. It is so much more! Our very physiology is wired up to falling in love. Being in relationship is a right way to live. *We are deprived if we don't.*

And – we are harmed if we have harmful relationships.

FORMS OF ATTACHMENT

Attached: The New Science of Adult Attachment and How It Can Help You Find – and Keep – Love provides information about research on Attachment Theory, and how couples can use it. The authors, Amir

Levine and Rachel Heller, give examples of three basic forms of attachment, and suggestions to improve relationships.

The first form of attachment is *Secure*, which is what we all want.

The second is *Anxious*. Those who develop this style are very sensitive to their partner and any indication that their security is threatened. They can appear clingy and needy.

The third is *Avoidant* Attachment. Many develop this style in order to *feel safe from their fear of love and commitment and dependency*.

Those with the more pronounced Avoidant style will have difficulty because they cannot allow themselves intimacy, transparency, and openness. Their dependence on a life separated into compartments makes it hard to integrate a lover. Deception feels normal, because they are accustomed to almost forgetting what goes on in the other compartments.

When couples understand their attachment styles they have an opportunity to take them into account. For example, if he knows he is Avoidant, and explains that to her, she will be less likely to take his behavior personally. She can ask him if he is shifting into Avoidant. If he can acknowledge it, they have a better chance of making it through conflicts instead of falling into circular arguments.

If she is Anxious she can monitor her emotions, express them to him, and at the same time, name that this is her Anxious style. This will help him not take her hurt and anxiety personally and thus be more able to provide what she might need to feel better. He may also set appropriate boundaries more calmly. In other words, *they can stay in the present instead of falling into old, false beliefs created by their childhoods and the culture*.

WHEN BOTH ARE SECURELY ATTACHED

Secures who mate with another Secure have an easier time resolving conflicts. They have better access to healthy approaches because they have experienced the comfort and safety they bring. They may get mad, want their way, have a lot of feelings, and criticize, but they start with a basic sense of trust in the relationship and each other. They know that life is secure, their relationship is safe, and they don't have to be defensive. Even if they feel shame they can balance it with relationship security.

If one partner steps outside of safe behaviors, such as flirting with a co-worker, or not calling when she said she would, he will not just act as if everything is all right. He will see that this isn't good for the Securely Attached relationship, feel threatened, and need to do something about it. He will want to ask her to help protect that Secure Attachment. He will bring it up, feel hurt or angry, and expect his partner to take a look.

Since she is Securely Attached she will, eventually, be able to understand and change her behavior. Or she will be able to explain what is going on so he will understand. She will do this not to be agreeable or cooperative, but because she sees that it is right when in a relationship.

She doesn't sacrifice. She doesn't compromise.
She understands.

She will have boundaries, too. If he is really upset over something she is doing that she knows is right for her to do, she will lovingly listen to his feelings, and then ask him to understand. She will explain that rowing three mornings a week with a team is supportive of her physical and mental health. She likes the team work. No, she isn't attracted to any of the men. And she is sorry that she can't stay in bed with him on Sunday mornings.

He doesn't like her choice, but feels secure because she has explained the importance of the activity. This kind of boundary-setting is essential in order for each person to maintain a sense of independent life. However, if it is defensively maintained, or the partner is blamed, it will impair the sense of security.

If we can see our own attachment style,
and that of our partner,
We will have a powerful way to understand
why we do what we do,
and why they do what they do.

The purpose isn't to have sympathy and let them off the hook, or to require change, but rather to *stay in the present, and thus less likely to feel upset.*

THE ANXIOUS AND THE AVOIDANT

Robert repeatedly asked his wife, Lily, to go do dinner at a new gourmet restaurant. The fourth time she said no, he lapsed into a silent, pouting mood. Without understanding his Anxious Attachment style, she was upset that he didn't understand why she couldn't go that night. Lily saw him as selfish and domineering, always wanting his way. She felt unloved, misunderstood and as if her needs were meaningless. So she went to her computer in the home office, ignoring what she perceived as his punishing pouting.

When Lily was able to understand that she was Avoidant and he Anxious, she could see how their approaches played off each other and created bad feelings. This brought her into the present, where she could set aside past hurts and needs. She could reach out to Robert instead of using her Avoidant way of responding to her mate's anger or disappointment.

She learned to turn to him and look him in the eyes. "Robert, I have something to say that I hope can help with this." When he was able to make eye contact and listen, she said, "I know that you really want to try the new restaurant, and I want to do that for you. I can't tonight, really, but let's set a date to do it, okay?"

Robert may not have been able to relinquish his hurt, and may have said, "You always say that! You want to put things off because you really don't want to be with me, do you? I've known for a long time that you prefer your co-workers to being with me. That really hurts."

Lily felt pulled to her Avoidance approach, and wanted to make a sound of disgust while walking away. But she hung in there. She could see that he saw her as powerful and controlling, and himself the poor victim of her choices.

"Robert, I don't like to be criticized for doing what I need for my job. Yes, I do like being with co-workers. And yes, I don't like being with you when you treat me badly and see yourself as my victim. I want you to understand what my job entails, and help me take care of the relationship, too. Going out to dinner tonight doesn't help us. It would make me tense and worried. I couldn't enjoy it. And you wouldn't like that either. Do you think you can hear my explanation of why I need to work tonight so we can get through this and still love each other?"

She may have shortened this into, "Please don't blame me because I have to take care of my job. It feels bad and puts me at a great distance from you."

When the Anxious Attacher, Robert, is able to step back and see his style of addressing conflict, he might handle it differently. He could say, "Babe, I'm feeling hurt that you don't want to do this simple thing I want to share with you. My Anxious Attacher is showing up here, and I'm feeling hurt and discounted. Can you give me some reassurance?"

Because his wife understands the needs of Secure Attachment, she could override her Avoidant style and tell him that she loves him, wants to go the restaurant with him, but she has to work one more night on a project that cannot be put off. She can offer to set up a weekend time.

The Securely Attached couple accepts that *anger is an appropriate emotion when used well*. Robert's wife can listen and nod when he says, "This pisses me off! I really want us to go out on a special date, and you keep putting me off. I don't really care if your boss needs you to put in all this extra time, I want you to make time for me, too. I don't want to compete with work. Aren't I first? Aren't I?"

Robert isn't criticizing. He isn't condemning. He isn't defensive. He isn't stonewalling. He is having *feelings*. Anger is natural when we don't get to have the relationship experience we want and need. But anger doesn't have to be used to control or criticize. His style invites Lily to feel loved and wanted. If she doesn't feel shamed by his comments, she will get to see that he is fully in the relationship, and she will want to have social experiences with him. He wants her! He likes being with her.

THE ANXIOUS AND THE ANXIOUS

Two people with anxious styles may be able to create a relationship that can work, based on taking care of each other. Both would focus on each other. This can actually guard their relationship as both would alert each other to interferences to their attachment.

Problems occur when one partner is less Anxious and begins to pull away. This can trigger the more Anxious partner into stronger anxiety, and make the couple look like the Anxious-Avoidant pairing. We each have in us the potential for all three styles.

Kim and Peter were highly attracted to each other when they met, quickly began sleeping together every night, and moved in together within a month. They planned their wedding, believing their relationship was it. But when Peter got a new job that he really liked, he started to have many of his relating needs met at work, and wanted less time with Kim. While this is a normal and healthy response, Kim was frightened.

She didn't know that she could explain her distress, feel it, and ask for his reassurance. So she cried and frowned and blamed him for her pain.

Peter felt guilty, tried to do what she needed, but of course failed. He cancelled the wedding and moved out the next month. Perhaps this was unavoidable given the strength of Kim's Anxious Attachment, but if they had understood the nature of Attachment styles, they would have had the chance to appreciate what was creating their emotions. They could practice new ways to handle them. Instead of blaming Peter, Kim could ask for reassurance. He could learn how to do that without sacrificing his new life at work. They could *protect their relationship* even when changes interfere with what they had created.

THE ANXIOUS AND THE SECURE

When an Anxious and a Secure mate it can work for them, too. The Secure will not be threatened by the neediness of the Anxious, and can easily offer reassurance. But along with reassurance, the Secure will retain comfortable boundaries around important issues. He or she will know not to sacrifice to make the Anxious feel safe, as that would create conflicts. Reassurance can help the Anxious feel more secure, and possibly become more secure.

THE AVOIDANT AND THE SECURE

This combination may permit the development of a good relationship, too. A Secure Attacher may be able to tolerate Avoidant behaviors without feeling too threatened.

However, if the Avoidant is too far down the Avoidance continuum, and is highly inaccessible, it is unlikely that the Secure would be satisfied with the relationship. Extreme Avoidants deprive their partners of solid attachment. A Secure is not likely to choose such a person for a mate.

THE AVOIDANT AND THE AVOIDANT

This combination can work when the manner of avoidance coincides. When both people work 80 hours a week, spending only a little time together, they are unlikely to encounter emotional needs that can't be met. However, even severe Avoidants have the same need and desire for a fully attached relationship, even if they resist it at the same time. This sets up a situation in which one or both want more from the other, even while not providing it themselves. Sexualizing with others, having affairs, and obtaining sexual stimulation including Internet porn can create the sense of having one's needs for love met. This is, of course, just an illusion.

Alcoholics and drug addicts can feel attached to each other over their use of alcohol or drugs. When one stops using, havoc can follow. Chapter 14 addresses how addiction can provide a facsimile of attachment. The addict is attached to the substance or behavior more than to the partner.

Ideally two Avoidants can study the nature of Secure Attachment and set out to work toward it. If they aren't too far along the continuum, they could find this an exciting project. Those with a more mild Avoidant approach to life can discover that they have a sense of independence that makes it easier to challenge their usually Attachment style. Anxious people, in contrast, must confront strong emotions that come with forgoing some of their overemphasized needs.

Chapter 6

Addiction and Love Attachment

Addiction actually comes under the heading of Avoidant Attachment, but deserves its own chapter. Active addicts cannot form a Secure Attachment to a person because their primary attachment is to the substance (alcohol, drugs, food, cigarettes) or the process (sexual stimulation, gambling, working, reading, worrying, etc.).

I'm using the word addict, but please include the use of substances and processes as drugs that command a good deal of energy even while the person does not qualify as addicted.

Addicts may be very dependent on a spouse or others, but not be able to engage in the supportive and reparative behaviors that are found in a well functioning relationship. In fact, the addiction, and the enabling of the addict, are what create the intensity common in relationships with addicts.

Addiction is composed of the *fantasy* of using, as much as the using itself. Unable to drink at work, she may imagine that glass of wine at the restaurant or in the refrigerator. She may think of her partner, but the scene is sharing a martini as they talk over their day. Wine connoisseurs think about preparing food – the food that goes with the particular wine. Many will find a recipe, buy the food, and carefully prepare it while opening that bottle of wine – the truly important component of the evening. Food addicts will enjoy the same process but the reward is the food itself. It isn't usually possible to eat all day but the awareness of the drug is always there.

The sex addict is aroused during the day over the idea that he will look at porn online when he goes home after work. When the addiction gets out of control he will go online while at work, threatening his job. Those whose addiction involves actually having sex will spend hours thinking about it. The activity itself takes little time compared to the day-long fantasy.

52

Imagine falling in love with someone who has his mind on something else all the time.

He is accustomed to that constant focus elsewhere while working, doing the wash, having conversations, and even having sex. If you drink or whatever with him he will appreciate combining his relationship with you and his addiction. But you don't come first.

ADDICTION ATTACHMENT

People who depend on a substance or process to alter their emotions are most often employing an Avoidant Attachment style of relating. While addicts may marry, and have strong feelings for their mate, they *depend on their drug for a constant, predictable, dependable source of feeling better.* Even when the addiction is to negative emotions, such as worrying, or criticizing, it still provides a sense of control over seemingly more painful emotions.

In contrast, for those who depend on a non-human attachment, falling in love is fraught with fear of loss, fear of betrayal, fear of criticism, and much more. The person could die, have sex with another, look at you with hatred, take an 80-hour-a-week job, or otherwise be uncontrollable. When you try to control, you will be met with either compliance accompanied by anger, or direct refusal to obey. This is all very disconcerting to those who want a smooth, orderly life with no major upsets. The addiction seems to provide this, only becoming a problem when it gets extreme or out of hand.

Addictions aren't this simple, of course. Our focus here is the choice between the unpredictable, *uncontrollable* nature of relationships, and the *seemingly predictable* nature of a substance or activity. Why not drink, eat, look at porn, use drugs, work a lot, gamble, scan and lust, exercise for hours, read volumes, talk nonstop, or any other compulsive activity in order to feel better? While these ways of controlling life can get out of control, and backfire, in the *fantasy* of using them, they are all good.

The majority of our population will use substances and behaviors for the *illusion of control* in their lives. Sadly, only a small percentage of people get to fall in love, feel incredibly sexual, not be able to keep their hands off each other, and find that the sex continues to get even better. A larger percentage can do the falling in love part, but the need to control one's shame with defensiveness, attack, frowns, criticism, contempt, and stonewalling pulls them away from the power of the sexual glue. Then sex becomes a need to be fulfilled at certain intervals, or becomes a seemingly pleasurable feeling that may bring affection with it. But it doesn't get to evolve into a deeply intimate, always changing interaction that gets better and better over time.

People who go into recovery from drug and alcohol abuse discover that they need to learn about love and connection, too.

While everyone professes to want love,
few realize that surrendering oneself to it
can be frightening.

If love and attachment weren't fully available in childhood, we will hold back, scrutinize, and move forward cautiously. Severe Avoiders might not be able to embrace them fully. Others of us go on to heal from a counter-productive style. We have to face the fear that can accompany transparent love.

Alcohol and drug treatment programs help with far more than recovery from substances. They *confront the Avoidant Attachment defenses*, and assist with the reduction of shame. It helps to address early life attachment deprivation and trauma, too, in order to claim all aspects of instinctive, wired-in needs for love and connection.

RECOVERING ADDICTS

Recovering addicts have to learn how to *shift their attachment from the addiction to people*. This may *sound* easy: just stop one thing and engage elsewhere. But it isn't. Most of us had less than perfect childhood attachments, so we fear the adult variety will be the same. The threat of placing one's emotional safety in the hands of another is unnerving.

Many of my recovering alcoholic clients no longer want sex with their partner. It had been easy when drinking because alcohol was primary and sexual loving was secondary. But sex can threaten one with feelings of chaos. Some people have affairs in order to split their attachment. The primary bond seems less threatening.

As a child with minimal attachment to my mother, I attached to the house we lived in. Other people attach to animals, to their room, to rituals, or to predictable household functioning. I dreamed about houses regularly for most of my life – houses that needed rooms and halls reorganized, which I would plan.

Those who attached to inanimate objects search for something that carries that needed constancy. Addicts who are exposed to an effective substance, such as alcohol, early in life find that it brings pleasure that resembles what they needed from birth and longed for in the arms of loved ones.

Studies show that high levels of childhood trauma are correlated with earlier and more extensive use of substances.

Since the experience of real life, especially when feeling love, is so much better than being under the influence of chemicals, we know that a high use indicates that something is very wrong.

Chapter 7

Men and Women and Shame

Men face unseen relationship issues that need special attention. Our culture doesn't let either gender see that *women are allowed to treat men badly*. We can shame them, shake our heads and frown over the simplest thing. Notice that in most commercials women put men down. Many sitcoms are based on it, too. Yet when I bring this up, most men will say that women rarely do shame them.

*Our culture blinds us to
how women shame men,
and what men do about it.*

MEN AND WOMEN NEED EACH OTHER TO UNDERSTAND

Blindness to the cultural shaming of men puts every relationship in danger. Blindness contaminates and also inhibits the best use of the rest of the practices in this book. If women blindly shame men, believing they haven't, they will not understand how they have contributed to irresolvable conflicts. If men don't see that women are shaming them, they won't understand why they react so strongly, and they won't be able to set boundaries around how they want to be treated. Understanding this difference will greatly improve the evolution of a new love.

SHAMING OF MEN

Here is a classic picture: Jim does something Marie finds unacceptable, such as not calling or coming late to dinner. Marie is exasperated and frustrated over being treated poorly, so she pouts, or in some other way puts Jim down. Jim doesn't like this, but thinks it's deserved. So he apologizes, or gets defensive, and in some way takes on the shame. One more layer is added to countless others.

But Jim can't just let this go. Even if he thinks he deserves it, it still feels terrible. His unconscious mind works on it, and the next thing he knows, he is doing something the culture believes is worthy of shaming again!

There are two reasons for this. One is to pay Marie back, even though he doesn't usually get to experience the revenge he seeks. The second is that as his shameful identity increases, there is really no reason to act in non-shame-worthy ways. It's like the child or teen from an abusive home who knows he will be treated badly by a parent whether he behaves or not, and so he has no reason to be "good." He acts within his identity of "bad."

The pattern with Jim and Marie continues. Once again, he has done something "wrong." She is justifiably frustrated, and punishes him with criticism and put-downs. All the communication in the world won't interrupt this pattern if it can't be recognized. Both people need to be able to see *how they shame*, and *how they are being shamed*, before they can stop this influence on relationships.

DIFFERENTIAL SHAMING OF MEN AND WOMEN

Our culture has many subtle ways of seeing women as the morally good gender, and men the bad. Because women are "good," it is more shocking when they do "bad" things than when men do. When you are aware that someone steals, you aren't too surprised to hear they did this shameful thing again. This is how we view men. But when a person you view as very honest steals, it is startling. Something must be terribly wrong for that to happen. This is how we view women.

While writing this chapter I walked through a parking lot and saw half a cigarette on the ground. Did a man or woman throw it there? I assumed it was a man. When we see a man do something that isn't politically correct we tend to shake our heads, and accept this as just the way men are. They do unappealing things like this. What's wrong with them? In other words, we shame them.

But if I were to see a woman throw down a cigarette, my reaction would be quite different. Expecting her to be less shame-worthy because she is a woman, I would be more shocked. And then I would judge her more harshly – I would wonder what was wrong with her.

While men get to belong to their gender when performing culturally shamed acts, women who do so are seen as far more shame-worthy. They don't properly belong to their gender. *The amount of shame women "deserve" is seen as greater than the man who does the same thing.* Men get to identify with their gender role of bad. Women, with the gender role of "good," are actually shamed more for evidence that they aren't true to their gender identity. Defining us as good actually casts more shame onto us than onto men.

ORDINARY SHAMING OF MEN BY WOMEN

I wrote a chapter in *Healing Humanity: Life Without Shame* called "Ordinary, Everyday Shaming." This is the kind that goes on all around us, and we don't recognize it as shaming. Here are some examples specific to love relationships:

•He reveals how he developed good communication skills in his high-level role in management. She says, "Why don't you do that with us?" Her tone says, what's wrong with you that you don't do that with us?

Instead, she could say, "I didn't know you had that expertise. Lets make use of it, okay?"

•Following her rules, he always tells her where he is going. He interrupts her business meeting to do so. She gives him a look that says, "You really should have had better judgment about when to tell me that."

She could have said, "Thanks," with no tone, and later explained that when someone is in her office, texting would be a good alternative.

•He excitedly tells her about the class he is taking on how to enhance his business. She very calmly says, "That's nice." Her tone says, "But what about all the other things you haven't done to increase your business?"

She might have said, "I'm happy for you. How did you find that class?"

58

•He asks his wife for sex. She slaps his hand away and makes shaming noises. He overhears her telling her friends that he wants it all the time and that's all men want.

She could sit down with him and explain that when he approaches her as if she is obligated, it prevents her from wanting sex. She could bring him a book to read together, or go to therapy, all offered in a reaching out vein instead of a critical one.

•He had used porn on the computer, had lap dances earlier in their marriage, and was going to 12-step meetings regarding his compulsive sexuality. He had not engaged in these activities for over a year. His wife randomly brought up the past and shamed him in a loud, angry tone.

If she understands that her reactions are 90% from the past, she will know that she needs to work on this in therapy and not attack her husband. She will be glad that he is changing.

•He tells her that he can't go to their daughter's recital because of a business meeting. She responds with, "How could you do that to your daughter?" You can imagine the tone because I don't think it's possible to ask this question in a non-shaming way. Another classic response is, "I just don't understand you."

She could respond with non-shaming anger, which is an appropriate emotion for her to have. She might say, "I don't like that you can't be there. This is more important than a meeting." Or she might calmly point out that she believes fathering includes being present when children are performing. And then accept that this is who he is. *Berating him for his choices will have no positive effect.*

•A woman brought her husband in for therapy because she said he was very controlling. He worked long hours and made a great deal of money, and also did much around the house. He sat quietly with a downtrodden look while she criticized him to me at great length. Many people would find this an acceptable scene: the bad, selfish, controlling husband and the poor, dominated, dependent wife.

As the scenes in the house were described, I could see that, actually, she was the controller. He did what he was told, and she complained that he didn't do it correctly.

I noted what I saw, and invited her to look at the possibility that actually, she was in control. She merely *felt* that she wasn't. This triggered her shame. She thought that I was letting him get away with his badness, and she was being held responsible. I tried to help her access the real feelings she was having about her marriage, and to consider the possibility that much of the emotion was from her past, but her shame prevented her from hearing much of what I said.

I became the object of her shaming. It turned out that I wasn't the good therapist she thought I was going to be. I didn't understand. I took his side against her. They were not coming back.

Seeing that I couldn't engage her, I was glad that her husband had one witness of the truth. I doubt that it did much for his high level of responsibility and shame, but I hoped he might find an individual therapist to assist him.

A man who walks away when he has been shamed too much would have left this woman long before. But this husband's history required him to stay. He apparently had different relationships with his mother and other childhood figures than avoidants who respond by leaving.

This husband didn't know that he didn't warrant his wife's treatment. His wife didn't know that she had real feelings that were projected onto her husband.

MEN GET WOMEN TO SHAME THEM

There are many ways that men trigger shaming reactions in women, usually with no awareness that they are doing so. (Women do, too, but I'm focusing on men here.) If we can come to see how we get people to shame us, we can change the pattern and receive less of the shaming.

•He thinks all day about calling her in response to her morning voice mail, but puts it off, justifying it by seeing himself as a procrastinator. When he calls her that night, he is already feeling shame for the delay. Added to this is his fear of her reaction. *He will feel shame whether she shames him or not.* Before she says anything, he defensively puts himself down for procrastinating.

•He can't tell her he is feeling unloved. All he can do is ask for sex for reassurance. He knows he is likely to be rejected, and this influences how he asks. She is turned off by the expression of neediness in his tone and facial expression and shames him for it.

• When he pouts over her refusal, she feels a combination of being repelled and guilt for not giving him what he "deserves." She predictably handles this with words, tone and body language that indicates he is just "one of those men" who only want sex.

• He promises her that he will complete paperwork for a project ASAP, but when he hasn't started in over a week, he knows she will be upset. Before she brings it up, he defensively complains that he hasn't had time and will get to it when he can. She doesn't even have to shame him for him to feel as if she has.

WHY DID YOU LEAVE RELATIONSHIPS?

Did you no longer feel good when around her? Did you not understand why? Did you have to make up a reason?

Brad said that he just didn't want to be there any longer, but until he learned about shaming he didn't understand that this is what drove him away. When he couldn't figure out why she complained about so many things, and when he just didn't know what to do about it, he gave up. He sees himself as an Avoidant Attacher. With no way to communicate about shame, he was taking care of himself in the only way he knew. He didn't know how to talk about their differences, and explain who he was, and what a partner could expect of him. This would have given the woman a chance to decide if his style was acceptable to her or not. Then instead of shaming, she could "select and then accept."

Brad's overall sense of inadequacy prevented him from reaching forward and communicating, knowing that he wasn't hurting anyone. Once he could understand how internalized shame altered his perception of himself, he saw how he accepted shaming without seeing it.

WHY COULDN'T YOU COMMUNICATE ABOUT SHAMING?

One simple answer is believing that you warrant it. You grew up being shamed, and this is more of the same.

It's just the way things are.

A second answer is that you did something wrong, and so you believe that it is correct to be shamed for it. *This is never the case.* You may have done harmful things, but healthy anger and sadness are the appropriate responses. You get to stop anyone who shames you, and demand that they present their information differently. Your very *shame identity* will encourage you to do shame-based acts that are not really in your integrity. If you take on even more shame, this isn't going to change.

Sadly, you may very well have unconsciously set yourself up by getting her to shame you. We humans have this odd way of playing out our histories by getting people to act like our parents and others from childhood. In order to prevent this, you will need to see how you do it so you can stop.

The primary answer to the question about why you can't communicate, however, is that *you don't even see it.* Bob and Susan both believed that Susan did not shame Bob. I saw many examples.

DIFFERENCES BETWEEN MEN AND WOMEN

•Men carry more overt shame than women. As I have said, the culture shames men more than women. We all believe that men are, in fact, shame-worthy.

Women's shame is covert; it is more hidden, and less visible to themselves and to men.

I have found it easier in therapy sessions and with friends to point out how the man is interfering with good relating than to point it out to the woman. She will feel far more defensive because she wants to believe that she is "good." Then she is likely to attack me or find another therapist. Men, on the other hand, already feel their shame, and accept criticism more easily. In contrast with women, their defensiveness will come from believing they are "bad."

While new love helps women feel good because shame falls away, it feels even better to men. Their shame is more visible to themselves, so getting to feel unconditionally loved is heaven. Then the fall is more painful, too. When she finds fault, and shames him, he will resort to old tactics to deal with it. He may try to *become really good*, he may *attack back*, or he may *pull away*.

•Men have more socially sanctioned methods of *hiding* shame, and of *sidestepping* their experience of it. Some of these include working hard, watching sports, animated impersonal conversations (such as about sports), and getting involved in projects. Male friends greet them with expressions such as, "She wasn't worth it anyway," or "There's plenty more fish in the sea," or "It was for the best." Back-slapping, taking him out to bars, or joking around serve to help the abandoned man not have to face his feelings. But then he has no one who really knows what he is going through.

•*Men are more devastated by relationship breakups than women.* Men don't typically reveal their pain the way women do. They tend to experience more anger than sadness, which brings activity instead of depression.

Men and women approach relationships and emotional healing differently. I offered a Meetup.com group called Relationship Skills Conversations and within two months had twenty-five women members and five men. The first meeting had all women, and we had a wonderful, intimate, lively exchange and agreed to keep meeting. When I offered an all-men's meeting, one man responded.

Men tend to be more Avoidantly Attached than women. I can give you my thoughts on why, but really, we just need to know it. So if you want a man in your life, you can learn how to present your non-negotiables before things get started, and when you feel he has agreed to them, accept him as he is.

THE GOOD AND BAD GENDERS

Our culture views women as the good ones and men as bad. Men are seen as not worthy of acceptance unless they are nearly perfect. They are not allowed to declare themselves deserving unconditional love and acceptance in the way women are. Western society views women as downtrodden and deserving to pull themselves up. Men are seen as having been given it all, and not using it well. They can't complain unless the economy is terrible and their business is failing. Women can still see it as their fault – even while sympathizing.

Men smoke cigars, watch sports for hours, drink, look at other women, don't call when late, don't call when expected to, tell dirty jokes, use sexual innuendos, flirt with others, rationalize to you, and put you down for objecting. They tell you they love you, that they love walking in the rain and snuggling on cold days by the fire, but do they ever do it?

For this we shame them.

MEN YEARN FOR LOVE MORE THAN WOMEN DO

Here's the irony. Men yearn for love and acceptance. They want to be held and looked at and see smiles. And at the very same time, they may pull away. Women see mixed messages, and react badly. So, women, here is why it is essential to understand what is going on inside an Avoidant Attacher. First he will want you, love you, value your touch. Then he will be so uncomfortable, he will pull away. He may do this by looking at other women, wondering if he made a mistake, and shifting isolating compartments. *Both attitudes exist at the same time.*

When the relationship ends, men are devastated. It is in the nature of Avoidance to be lonely and separate emotionally from others, even while spending a lot of time around people. The love relationship provides a facsimile of connection that is difficult to relinquish.

Another irony: women are the same. We yearn for that loving man who will look at us with affection, give us warm hugs and love-making, and put us first. And then when he does, *we look for everything wrong with him and tell our friends about it.*

We expect men to know what we want and how a relationship should unfold, and then feel hurt when they don't do it right.

I spoke with a single man in his 50's who had been through a series of relationships that just seemed to peter out. He said that his partner would turn cold or distant, and he didn't know why. He just didn't know why. After reading this book he came up with some ideas of what he might say instead of just letting her walk away. He didn't realize that he might have asked her what was wrong, or what had he done.

Women, a man will yearn for you as he yearns for the love he didn't receive as a child. The more empty he feels, the harder he will yearn. But once you give him your full love, attention and affection, he could very likely pull away from you. First, you will never be the mom he never had. Second, you will begin finding fault and then look like the mom he did have. And third, he may find the intimacy threatening and come up with reasons for why he has to pull back.

Women need to know that the extent of his yearning
doesn't correlate with the extent to which
he wants you or loves you.

A number of men yearned for me when it was very clear that they didn't know me at all. One man with whom I ended a brief affair would look at me in meetings with such full-out adoring, yearning expressions that I would feel it physically. Yet we both knew that his level of avoidance prevented a relationship. He knew I wasn't for him, but his emotions of deprivation took over anyway.

In my 20's, before I had any understanding of relationships, I had a college friend whose boyfriend begged her to marry him. She wasn't comfortable with his urgency, but several of us envied her for having a man so in love. We told her that she should accept his proposal. She did. When we saw her more than a year later, we heard about how he had pulled away, and had little interest in her or their relationship. I was appalled and felt guilty for encouraging her to marry him. Now I understand that he was a strong Avoider, and as long as she held back, he yearned for her. But once she came forward, he shifted into Avoidance.

Women know they have intense feelings about men, but since men don't talk about theirs, we aren't aware that they feel even more strongly than we do. Women typically have friendships that allow processing the feelings, which makes these emotions more visible to us.

PULL PUSH

It doesn't start with the push, it begins with pulling each forward. I had an interesting conversation with a married man who isn't, of course, dating. He was fascinated by my ability to read his energy and quickly agreed to being interviewed for a book I plan to write on Avoidant Attachment. In the first hour he poured out the details of his relationship history, including having affairs and buying prostitutes. I was amazed that he trusted me enough to do this, but chalked it up to my specialization in sexuality because he knew that I have already heard it all.

In our second interview a week later, he pulled back. He sounded reluctant to talk and was glad to quickly end the conversation when I had what I needed.

He was a severe Avoider, and because of it, even while in a long-term marriage, he yearned for closeness and connection. If I did not understand this, I wouldn't have known why he pulled back.

If he were my lover, I would have reacted mostly out of my history. I might have felt bereft and criticized and tried to get him to come close. And then he would have had to figure out how to deal with my pursuit, how to pull away.

Chapter 8

The Power of Sexual Glue

Sex is the third of the five arenas in which new couples can preserve their relating. When sex is used as a relationship glue, a couple can be off to a great start!

We will take a look at the function of sex in making a relationship special and secure, and how monogamy is far more than not having sex with others. Then we can address those obstacles to using sex this way. As obstacles are removed or healed, each partner will become freer to use this marvelous power for its intended purpose.

Love, intimacy, transparency, honesty, touch, empathy,
time, attunement, caring conflict resolution, and
co-creating of life together make up the foundation for
the truest monogamy.

Isn't this amazing? Sex is so much more than activities that merely feel good. So much more than meeting a physical need. So much more than demonstrating love.

Sex activates the coupling attachment!

MONOGAMY

Monogamy is usually defined as having a sexual relationship with only one person for a period of time. It typically includes the omission of sexual activity with others. This view of relationships and marriage is portrayed in religious teachings and is inherent in our cultural values.

But *true inside-out monogamy is far more*!

Cultural damage has prevented most people from discovering the full purpose of sex, and thus the easy and desired limitation of the outside-in use of it.

Sex is relationship glue!

The creation of an exclusive bond starts right from the first flirtation. If someone flirts with you, you don't want him or her to flirt with someone else. This is in contrast to friendship, in which relating with several people can be even more enjoyable than talking with just one.

If we know how to understand and protect the relationship glue, we can greatly enhance the relationship. The classic American belief is that the first year includes lots of sex, and then it predictably drops off. Couples say that won't happen to them, but then it does. And they don't know what to do about it. Allowing the powerful influence of sex to fall away can be prevented by taking good care of the relationship.

TALK BEFORE, DURING AND AFTER

Couples can start right out talking about sex. Getting acquainted with each other's experiences and preferences can reduce the embarrassment of talking when they are engaging in sex. Instead of thinking that sex is something you just do, and it either goes okay or not, we can set out to embrace this vital arena of falling – and staying – in love.

My book, *Reclaiming Healthy Sexual Energy: Revised*, explains how individuals can heal their damaged sexuality. The first half addresses individual healing, and includes the vast role of the culture in defining sexuality in harmful ways. The second half shows couples how to work together to claim their sexuality. I identify all the cultural influences that harm the natural unfolding of a couple's sexual relating. If you are able to see them, it becomes easier to avoid the harm. For example, the idea that sex isn't complete unless both people are aroused and reach orgasm inhibits the natural unfolding of whatever sexual activity is right for that time. Perhaps lots of kissing is right one time, oral sex another, and intercourse another. Or perhaps all three are correct. You find out by what seems natural to do next, not by a plan or requirement.

Please read my book before dating as there isn't room here to provide the necessary information. You will learn about a new approach to engaging sexually, one that is free of rules and views of sexuality that are approved by the culture.

SEX AND DATING

We all know that when we are dating, sex is right there in front of us. Is she attracted? Is he flirting with me? Is he going to kiss me? Does he kiss everyone he dates? What does it mean if he wants to kiss? What does it mean if she wants to have sex?

HEALING THE GLUE

Even though sex in the well-attached relationship shouldn't decrease, in this sex-crazy culture we have to do a lot to maintain the glue effect. We can remove the influences of those around us and the media. And we can heal from past damage, the inappropriate addressing of our sexuality while growing up. We can see what the culture believes is correct, and reject those parts that aren't.

Chapter 9

When the Present Looks Like the Past – but Isn't

We form much of our view of life and the world around us from our early interactions with adults. If we have a Secure Attachment with our mother, and then others, we believe the world is safe and our needs will be met. If we were neglected or abused, we expect neglect and abuse as the years go on.

Our adult task is to figure out what we have
projected onto the present from those old experiences.

This will help us see what is actually happening now, and what is made up from the past.

Getting the Love You Want, by Harville Hendrix, explains how we take childhood experience and transfer it onto the present. He explains how we select our partners, and how we relate with them, based on childhood relationships.

Differentiating between what is going on right now from what happened in the past can be difficult. We have been conditioned to respond to charged situations, and that conditioning takes over even when it is not actually occurring in the present. Here is a rule of thumb that might help:

When you are having strong feelings,
start with the assumption that
only about 10% is from the present, and
the rest is left over from some other time.

My friend Susan really doesn't like it when her boyfriend, Bob, is "gone." This means that his mind and emotions are off somewhere else and he isn't available to her. His hugs feel like furniture. He doesn't make eye contact. He reacts defensively when she asks where he has gone. He tries to be playful, but it fails.

We all retreat at times. We aren't any fun to be around, and we don't like being that way much ourselves. But the mood ends, and we come back.

Susan knows that when I fall into the past, she is okay. But when Bob does, that triggers her childhood memory. Remember all those intense emotions I described in Chapter 2? Here they come. She is sure he will leave forever, and she wants to pull away from him (Avoidant behavior). She feels abandoned, and then angry about it. She will quiz him or scold him, but of course it has no effect. Bob cannot just magically decide to get out of his mood.

THE 90% GUIDELINE

It can be helpful to understand that only a small percentage of the strong emotion triggered by a partner is really about what is going on in the present. It can feel better if you know that the intensity of our reaction is not about what we have done, it's about something else.

We can assume that about 10% of Susan's emotional response is from actually missing her lover. It's nicer to have dinner and spend the evening if he is present. Of course she knows how to have her own evening separate from him and can elect to do that.

The other approximately 90% comes from childhood where her mother and other family members were so focused on their own emotional pain that they had no attention to spare for Susan. Since she was a child, she truly needed that attention. She figured out how to get negative responses from her parents, and at the same time, she maintained the belief that she deserved more even if it weren't available.

Since our lovers are seen as a stand in
for the parent who couldn't provide what was needed,
we project those needs on to him or her.

Now well loved by Bob, Susan experiences childhood abandonment, triggered by his emotional "abandonment."

Her job is to understand that he hasn't caused her pain. He only caused mild disappointment. The pain is left over, a relic of her past. If she knows this, and can remember it during the experience of feeling left, then she can heal from the pain of the past!

Since I am a close friend, Susan might call me to walk her through it. I will ask her what she is feeling and when she felt that way during childhood. As she ponders the emotion and its history, she will add another piece to her understanding. Perhaps she will remember another event when her mother turned away from her. She might recall how her mother was so distressed over her husband's lack of attention, she had little perception of her children's needs. Or she might have a vague sense of being left alone too long in her crib. Once she can cry over those ancient experiences, she will increasingly be able to see that Bob hasn't actually left her. He just goes off into his emotional issues, so to speak, and can't relate well for a while. Don't all of us do what Bob does?

The 90/10% split is of course arbitrary. It could be 50/50%, or even 10/90%. As my healing from childhood trauma progresses what was a 90% historical reaction gradually lessens until it becomes merely a 10% mild sense of discomfort. And then it can become no percent at all! Or it can be zero one time, and then up to 25% the next, depending on my state, what the trigger is, and who I am triggered by.

COMPASSION FOR PARENTS

While we do have to examine the deficiencies and abuses in our childhood, at the same time we can have understanding of our parents who didn't know what was needed. Although we may not have had seriously abusive or neglectful parents, most of us were deprived by their gentle neglect. They may have been distracted by their own emotions and needs, or were otherwise not entirely available to us. No one is ever entirely available to us, and we all have to learn to accept that. We don't have to lay blame.

I became depressed when my son was born, which launched my study of psychology. I couldn't help it, and consequently my son was deprived. I did the best I could, but I wasn't able to pay complete attention to his needs. I have compassion for myself, and sadness for this, as I do for those parents who were unable to understand what we needed. We can assume that most parents want to be good parents, but their own histories *and our culture* interfere.

OLD PAIN

Falling in love triggers all of that old un-grieved-for pain because coupling is our most powerful form of adult attachment. If we dealt with childhood attachment deprivation by becoming Anxiously Attached, running after the parent, crying and demanding to be taken care of, then we are likely to respond to a partner's pulling away with similar approaches. But if we took care of ourselves by shifting into an independent, Avoidant sense of life (false, but effective), then we are likely to deal with intense pain by pulling back.

In the beginning of her love affair with Bob, Susan would tell him that she didn't think she could cope with his emotional leaving, his "being gone," and that she didn't know if she could continue the relationship. I explained that this threatens any partner and actually encourages him to pull away even more. It certainly doesn't invite him to come forward.

I pointed out that *when she was "in memory" of her childhood, she wasn't able to think clearly about the present.* If she thought for a period of time about whether or not she wanted to be in a relationship with Bob, and decided the answer was no, then it would be appropriate to tell him it was over. But to threaten it in the heat of emotion was cruel. In her need to feel safely in retreat, she hurt him with abandonment. Susan understood this, and made sure to never do it again. Instead, she tried to assure him that she wasn't leaving even when she felt like doing so.

It's better to have friends who understand the 90/10 division of the causes of emotion than to call someone who says, "Yeah, that guy is just an idiot, you should get rid of him. Who does he think he is to treat you like that?" Or, just as unhelpful, "Think about what you did to get him to react like that." Some mental health and recovery practices encourage people to look at how they are responsible. Occasionally this can help, but I believe we need to see how our reaction to any real or imagined hurt is a reflection of true attachment neglect or abuse in childhood. If we start with this premise we will have a constructive course of action in front of us.

PARTNERS MAY SAY
OBVIOUSLY HURTFUL THINGS.

If you use the 90/10 rule, you can see that perhaps only 10% of the hurt or anger comes from shaming comments, while the intensity belongs to the past, accounting for the remaining 90%.

Some examples of hurtful things partners may say:

You're stupid.
What you did was so ridiculous.
I can't believe you are wearing that.
I'm going to divorce you if you do that again.
What's wrong with you?
You hurt me so much!
I can't ever trust you.

If you were responding to only the 10%, you would react with emotion and also with understanding. You could tell your partner that you feel hurt. You could ask her or him to say it again in a non-hurtful way. You would be able to see that such hurtful statements preclude intimacy. You could see that you need to take care of yourself and not receive any more negativity.

If your partner repeatedly levels this kind of statement at you, you might ask yourself if this relationship is acceptable. You might plan to leave. Or you might find a therapist who could help you understand a relationship system that both of you are engaged in. Once you understand, then you would know how to handle it.

CIRCULAR ARGUMENTS

That 90% can make everything seem unbearable. The hurt feels deep and impossible to heal. You can't turn around and leave, but you can't stand to stay either. So you put it back on her or him. You criticize, or you put him down to hurt him back. Then his 90% gets him to do the same to you. Around and around you go, and as the hurts pile onto one another you lose sight of the original issue, that first thing you did that she put you down for, that first discomfort, that first shame.

Understanding how this works is one of the vital components to helping a relationship develop well.

EMOTIONS PAST AND PRESENT

The emotions described in Chapter 2 are strong because they are intensified by the sexually bonded relating. This makes sense when we understand that when we fall in love our hormones and brain functioning are similar to that of mothers and infants. We literally feel as if we are the infant and our partner is the essential grownup. That is really intense, isn't it? This is why we need to respect the nature of the connection that is formed. It is also why

we need to understand how much of what we feel
was actually created in our childhood, and
no longer exists in the present.

When I feel intense hurt, or longing, or abandonment, it seems to make sense in my present life. But if I think that's true, then many around me are not at all nice people. They seem worthy of being eliminated from my life! But if I understand that they had depriving childhoods, too, then I can consider that nothing all that horrible is going on right now.

A man I dated had a habit of being mean in very small ways. He would pretend that he hadn't heard what I said, or when I asked a question would look right at me and not say anything. He would tell me critical things someone else had said about me when it was clear that he had set them up to say it. These fall into the category of passive aggressive behaviors, and can be read about in *Living with the Passive Aggressive Man*, a book by Scott Wetzler.

The answer seemed simple. He was bad. I was harmed.

But when I looked at it through the 90/10 filter, my perception changed. I could know that he was angry, perhaps at me and at his parents, and he didn't know how express it directly. He didn't know that having had controlling parents left him angry because he rationalized that their excessive control was for his own good. He was unable to address his meanness, though, and eventually I ended it.

FRIENDS AND LOVERS

When Susan told me that she hiked with an old friend from years past, I was puzzled over why I had not met this friend. I had not even heard about her. I felt a little left out, wanting to believe I knew everything about my best friend's life. Why hadn't she told me?

My emotions were far less intense than they would have been with a partner, but it gave me a chance to experience the 90/10 in a manageable way. I could ask myself how I had been left out in my childhood. One obvious answer is that as an Avoidant Attacher, I got myself left out. It served its function, even while leaving me alone and unseen. This is what I was working on healing. The remaining ten percent was no more than curiosity about Susan not having mentioned this other friend.

So I asked. She filled me in. I got to affirm that my friend was actually transparent, which is how we are. I was back "in the present" instead of somewhat "in memory."

If this had been with a lover, my concern would have been far stronger, but I could have handled it the same way. I wouldn't have quizzed him about his friend. Instead I would have said that I was feeling left out and a little afraid, could he please fill me in? He would of course understand 90/10 because I would have explained it all before we became lovers. Perhaps he would have had his own 90/10 in reaction to feeling accused, and then we would have to *figure out how to name both of our 90's and both of our 10's*. Once we could see clearly, then we could also see what each of us needed in order to feel solid again.

Some reactions are 100% history. One of these is sexual experiences, which can actually be entirely from memory. Sexual shaming and abuse in childhood can result in adults wanting to not be sexual, or preferring to be sexual in a manner that does not support love and intimacy. Their partners may think they are unloved or unattractive or unwanted. When they can see that the disinterest has nothing to do with them, it can be easier to tolerate.

GRIEVING FREES US FROM THE PAST

Once we can see distortions in our current thinking and feeling, we have the opportunity to grieve them away, much as we grieve for the death of loved ones, with anger and protest, along with tears, and then letting go.

If we had been able to grieve for our childhood hurts back when they happened, they wouldn't be carried into the present. But we weren't. First, we were too young to tolerate those intense emotions. And second, most of us were told not to cry or be angry, thus inhibiting those very needed healing emotions.

Going back to the example of my best friend having a friend I knew nothing about, I could use this situation to grieve for the fact that I essentially lived outside of my family. I could remember taking our dog for a walk and feeling isolated and alone on a trail through the forest. Or being with the other girls in the neighborhood and knowing I didn't fit in and belong. I hadn't been able to learn how because my dedication to being invisible prevented it. I could shake my head with compassion for that young person I was. I could understand that fantasizing about finding a man to make everything perfect would be a natural approach to feeling better. I was so isolated, I couldn't set out to actually find a boyfriend to provide this until much later. But even if I had found one, my mother prevented me from dating.

By wonderful contrast, my dear friend sat in front of me, looking right at me, and explained why I hadn't heard about her friend. I could shift right into the present, know I was loved, and that she wasn't keeping part of her life away from me.

This is how we heal!

Deep friendships, group therapy, 12-step meetings, and other gatherings can provide a sharp contrast to the experience of being raised by parents who were abusive or didn't know how to parent. A love relationship can potentially provide this contrast, too. However, the triggering of strong emotions on both sides can actually prevent using the relationship to heal the past. When our partner responds as if he or she has been hurt by our projection, it can seem to actually re-play the childhood experience.

If my friend had been, instead, my lover, he might have felt assaulted by my response to his unnamed friendship. He could have frowned and told me I was being suspicious for no reason. He might have said that he did tell me about her, that my memory was the problem.

Then what would I feel? I might have wondered if he were trying to keep something from me. I could have felt jealous or frightened when it was just his shame over feeling unjustly accused.

Our long range goal is to understand the typical emotions triggered in ourselves, and then in our future partners, so that they can be seen for what they are. If I knew he would feel accused, I could preface my questions by telling him that what I was about to say could sound accusing. Then he would be able to watch out for this emotion, knowing it was at least 90% history.

But still, it would be much harder than with my friend. I am quite sure that she had no motivation to hide something from me. Why would she? It's not who she is. But even the *thought* of a lover hiding something brings discomfort. My fears could bring suspicious questions such as: Why does he have to go off into those compartments? If he can so easily hide this casual friendship, what else can he hide? Are his compartments so easily entered that he could "accidentally" fall into an affair and not realize that it will destroy us?

If he explained in an entirely reassuring manner, I would feel great relief. With Susan I smiled and felt a little silly. *Love relationships are so much more volatile.* Of course they are, because they represent those very attachments that we needed to survive as babies and children. Yes, *actually survive.* Babies who feel too much disconnection and lack of attachment will die. This was recorded in orphanages in France during WW II. Babies were cleaned, fed, and kept warm in cribs, but they died until it was discovered that volunteers spending loving time with them kept them alive. (Google Rene Spitz for more information).

If you experience a need at this level of survival, and project it onto your mate, a lot of emotion is bound to come along with it! You can actually feel as if your life is in danger, even while you intellectually know that it isn't. This is where

> *protecting the relating, and learning how to repair hurt,*
> *are needed in order to*
> *create the most supportive loving relationships.*

When this is integrated into the relationship, both partners can actually heal the harmful effects of their past.

DISCOVERING CHILDHOOD PROJECTIONS

Appendix A has a list of questions that can help you take a look at what may have gone on during childhood that you are projecting onto the present. It can be an initial tool to help you learn about yourself.

A second approach is to look at adult relationships you have formed in order to see the kind of people you choose. Even when we think the new person is entirely different from past partners and dates, there are common elements that can be discovered. Take a look at how you misperceived your partners based on childhood needs.

For example, you may be with a person who is quite attentive to your real needs, yet still, you feel as if he or she isn't. When you project childhood onto your mate, he or she may seem to be like your parent. Then you get to explore to see how much he is like your parent, and how much you have made up. Did you *select* someone like the parent, or did you *come to believe* that she was?

Mapping out your projections and partner choices are complicated tasks, best done with others. Individual therapy, group therapy, or a gathering of friends offer environments in which everyone can learn about their projections. It is helpful to have a sub-culture of others where it is routine to question the role of the past in our present behavior. At the very least, shame for current behaviors is reduced because you get to see that *it wasn't your fault*!

You are now left with the responsibility for no longer giving in to those projections. But, still, they aren't your fault.

ADDICTION TO HOPE

The next chapter explains how *hope* and *expectation* are the outcome of projections from our past, and from the culture. So many of us believe that if we just find the right person, if we just fall in love, then the relationship will unfold appropriately. When it doesn't, we are likely to fall into blaming, shaming, and controlling.

Acceptance means seeing who the person is, really learning about him or her, and then deciding if this is someone you can be with. If not, don't start. If you start, then accept.

Chapter 10

The Danger of Hope and Expectation

Expecting others to be the way we have made them up to be, and focusing on hope for them to change, rather than seeing how they are, are powerful obstacles to healthy relationships.

I suggest asking each potential partner to read this book, and discuss each concept together. This will help you avoid falling for someone who just wants nice relating with no understanding of the pitfalls.

For example, a man I dated whom I will call David thought I was pretty wonderful, and he wanted to hold my hand and kiss right away. I asked him if he were willing to read books on relationships and get more in touch with his emotions, as he was an engineer with the classic intellectual approach to life. He leaned toward me and said Yes, he would do what it took.

In a very few weeks I could see that he was a strong Avoider, and couldn't leave his compartments for very long in order to relate with me. At that time I still thought that if I could just explain, just communicate, that the other person would embrace my understanding and change. He tried. But it was too much to ask. After decades of separating his life into compartments, he could just not step out of them and enter a Securely Attached relationship.

If I had already written this book, and asked him to read it, it would have become clear to me before ever getting started that he wasn't a candidate for the full-out relationship I wanted. He would have been able to see that I wasn't right for him, too. He treasured his compartments. He needed to keep other aspects of his life separate from his love life. If he had known what I wanted, he would have run in the other direction!

Hope addiction is a concept from the world of addiction recovery. It is a focus on the future instead of understanding what is right in front of us.

It prevents us from assessing accurately
because it is looking forward to what
we think the other person can do or become.

We may try to change them, educate them, get them to the right helping professionals, get them into addiction recovery, or in some way control them into what we think they should be. Shaming is integral. When the hope addict shames, the recipient will usually shame back. Again we have the circular argument, the circular shaming.

Some of the countless changes we want from our partner are: more sex, less sex, more talking, less talking, more done around the house, the right things bought from the store, less drinking, weight reduction, more affection, less clinging, earning more money, working for longer hours, not lying, not flirting, not arguing, not shaming, not exhibiting passive aggressive behavior such as admiring the looks of another person, and taking out the garbage.

Add your own. What have you wanted a partner to change? What have they wanted you to change?

ASKING FOR CHANGE

Of course these issues can be addressed. You can ask your partner to change them. These may be conflicts that you can learn to resolve constructively. But if your partner can't or doesn't want to change, then what?

BOUNDARIES ARE NEEDED

Boundaries are next. You get to stop being around behaviors that interfere with your life. You can ask her to stop talking for now, because you need quiet. You can express distress when he flirts in front of you.

What you mustn't do is shame or badger him or her into being different.

You mustn't stay around, or keep confronting, just because you believe that he or she will just change if you can figure out how to do enough, how to help, or how to bully them into it.

The man I will call Stan was different from David. He didn't hurt me. He was clear that he was such an Avoidant that neither of us would want us to be together. But I wanted to change him anyway! I interviewed him regarding his Avoidant style, I educated him, I asked him questions about his parents and how they treated him in childhood. I interpreted his dreams.

But Stan had not once shown an interest in healing these obstacles to a fully committed relationship! I alternated between being angry that he didn't have the courage to take on the healing, and feeling deeply grieved over having to leave him back there in Avoidance while I graduated into the ability to attach fully.

I couldn't just decide to stop doing that. What I could have done was to carefully evaluate at the beginning so I knew what I was getting into. Then when I saw the remnants of the desire to change someone, I could talk about it! And have the needed emotions to heal it.

I have three woman friends who don't want live-in relationships. They want occasional lovemaking and companionable time with a partner. They might relate more comfortably with either of these men because they are more alike in what they want. These women may not try to change them!

First select. Then accept.

If you cannot accept, then get help with your emotions so you don't impose them on your partner.

Chapter 11

Exploring Your Conflict Resolution Style

We're going to take a closer look at the four conflict resolution styles that have been established as highly detrimental to relationships. John Gottman, author of *The Seven Principles for Making Marriage Work*, found that he could watch couples having an argument in his observation room and within thirty minutes predict if they would divorce. He had an accuracy rate of over 90%.

We all have conflicts, and we need to resolve them.
We can use old ways that drive partners apart,
or we can replace them with a healthy expression of
wants, needs, and emotions.

The first step is taking a look at your typical approaches, both the effective and the ineffective. You may depend on one, or use many. Once you can see how you may block an easy route to resolving conflicts, then you are ready to practice new, better approaches. The new ones will not push your partner away. They will invite her to come forward to work with you.

I . DEFENSIVENESS.

Defensiveness is a common response to feeling shame.

Defensiveness is a pervasive attempt to avoid feeling shame. It is used by pretty much everyone having been built into our culture. It may be triggered when one partner brings up a conflict that appears to be finding fault. I wrote a chapter in *Healing Humanity: Life Without Shame* on how we use defensiveness in ways that are counter-productive.

You can see which examples of defensiveness ring true for you. (The next chapter has suggestions for what else to try.)

<u>Victim approach</u>. Seeing yourself as the victim of the other person will not lead to working together to resolve something. Instead, it leads to circular arguments. A tries to describe something he didn't like. B is triggered into feeling like a victim, and says, No I didn't, you are wrong, and you are hurting me by suggesting it. Then A gets triggered, says, Wait, I'm not wrong, you are. And around and around it goes.

<u>Proving the other is wrong</u>. Going online for studies proving his point, skewing the choice of sites, quoting friends' statements that he is right, and using "logic" will not end the conflict. Somehow if he can prove her wrong she will have to give in. Still, the conflict remains.

<u>Rationalization</u>. This involves giving elaborate reasons that are superficial, and not the real explanation, for behavior that he or she isn't comfortable revealing. People can believe their own rationalizations.

Rick explained that his lover should accept his drinking because she knew when they met that he was a wine connoisseur and that alcohol was an integrated part of his life. He pursued this thinking even when she pointed out that she hadn't known that he abused alcohol and blacked out. When she named this, he acted as if she were being critical and inappropriate.

Examples of rationalization:

• An accident slowed traffic, and I tried to call but my Bluetooth wasn't working properly.
• I forgot. (Sometimes true, but can be motivated by something else.)
• I didn't know I had that man's phone number on my contacts list, I don't know how it got there.
• I wasn't looking at that woman's breasts, I was admiring her clothes.
• I didn't like when he touched my arm like that, but I didn't want to hurt his feelings by telling him to stop.

•But I had to buy her that drink. She said she was thirsty and we were sitting at the bar.

•I got your message this morning but I just didn't get around to calling you back until tonight.

•I didn't spend that money; you didn't read the credit card statement right.

Sometimes tone of voice may suggest that they are rationalizing or lying because they feel defensive, when they are actually telling the truth.

2. CRITICISM

We have seen everyone around us, from our parents, teachers, and television to churches, making it acceptable to tell someone that they are bad in some way.

Some examples of criticism are:

•You always think of yourself.
•You never think of me, do you?
•You are such a slob.
•You're a liar.
•You should have known better.
•You are so stupid.
•Why do I bother staying with you?
•I just can't believe you could think that way!
•What were you thinking?
•You're fat and ugly.
•No one would ever want to have sex with you.
•No one else would want to be in a relationship with you.
•You always hurt me.
•Get it together. Do you think I'll wait forever?

Sweet criticism can be more difficult to detect. What about when she looks at you with doe eyes and sighs. She might say something like, "I want to help you change, really I do. But I just don't know how." Or, with head shaking and more sighs, "I try so hard, but I just don't seem to

88

be able to get through to you." This can appear to be genuine concern, but it's just another way of saying something is wrong with you.

3. CONTEMPT

Contempt escalates the tone and facial expression turning criticism into total condemnation.

- You are such a piece of shit!
- You don't belong on this earth.
- What*ever* made you think that you should have said anything?
- I can't believe you thought you had something valuable to say.
- You look like shit.

Contempt is a total discounting, down-putting attitude that suggests an impossible relationship. It predicts divorce. If the person leveling contempt alternates it with expressions of love and need, it creates confusion. The partner is set up for a kind of brainwashing about her perception. How could someone who condemns her also love her? If she believes the love, as we tend to once we are attached, she is likely to believe the contemptuous phrases, too. This is emotional abuse that accumulates over time.

If you express contempt, notice the sensation in your chest, how you swell up, feel powerful, and enjoy the fact that the other person is powerless even if they object. There is no defense against contempt. If she protests, you just laugh it off.

Think about the reason you feel the need for this kind of power. Are you sick of his or her victim attitude? Does she act like you are always hurting her? Does he demand your attention all the time? Have you just had it? You may need help practicing how to use healthy anger instead.

4. STONEWALLING

When issues seem impossible to resolve, some people will pull back into Avoidance and stop talking. This may include pouting and expressing criticism with facial expressions. Such behavior has been described as a grey cloud, a black cloud, negative energy pervading the house, or sucking all the energy out of the room.

Stonewalling can take the form of leaving without saying when she will be back, turning a cold shoulder while engaging in normal activities, or acting as if questions haven't been asked.

When parents stonewall, it can trigger fear of abandonment and resulting Anxious Attachment and protest behaviors. Being shunned is extremely painful. Solitary confinement is the most psychologically devastating form of punishment. When occurring in a relationship, it brings on not just historical pain, but also current, instinct-driven human need for connection.

Stonewalling needs to be differentiated from healthy space-taking in the midst of intense arguing. One partner can say, "I'm going to go upstairs to the office so we can calm down. I'll come back in a while." Or, "I'm going to leave for an hour, but I will be back. Talking isn't going to lead anywhere when we feel like this."

The partner will often object to the leaving, and criticize, but he needs to take the space anyway. It may look like abandonment, when in fact it is a healthy break from something that cannot go forward at that time.

IDENTIFYING YOUR STYLE

You might find it useful to begin making a list of examples of your conflict resolving styles. Focus on each one, reflect over what you have said to others, and how it felt.

Since every one of us carries shame,
every one of us will be accustomed to using
at least one of these four harmful styles.

Knowing that everyone else does it too can sufficiently free you from shame so that you can take a look. You can only begin to change something that you can perceive. Here again, working with a group of people can relieve shame and provide the best education.

The next chapter addresses approaches to changing your conflict resolution style.

Chapter 12

Identifying and Changing Your Conflict Resolution Style

Since conflict brings up feelings of shame for most people, taking a look at that emotion comes first. How do you feel when criticized? When your partner doesn't like something you do? It feels bad, doesn't it? You want to get him to change his mind as quickly as possible. So you resort to methods that you have long employed – even though they may not work.

Criticizing back or looking upon her with contempt
doesn't invite her to pay attention to how you are feeling.

The only chance for this to go well is if you look her in the eyes and tell her that this is making you uncomfortable. And then continue the conversation – *slowly!*

Observe!

This is the first step in any change you want to make. Observe:
•what you do,
•how you feel,
•what you want to say, and
•what you do say.

This will show you what you want to change.

Notice your emotional reaction–that strong sense of her being wrong, of your being right, and of angrily wanting to make this entirely clear. Instead, why not allow yourself to feel some shame? Discover that it is just a feeling. You aren't really a horrible person because he doesn't like something you did. Even if he tells you that you are a horrible person, you still get to know that you aren't!

When Susan swore at Bob, he lapsed into hurt and withdrawal. He felt such shame that he couldn't imagine any future for the two of them. He said that he felt hated and worthless – in other words, shame about his very being. As we talked about this, he gradually came to see that his parents' treatment of him was the cause of this devastating emotion. He could be angry with Susan for swearing at him, but she didn't see him as worthless. She didn't want to get rid of him.

Bob knew that if he shamed Susan back by acting like her victim, he could reduce his own experience of it. Once he could recognize his emotion, then he could use it more constructively.

Once you have shame under control,
changing your conflict resolution style
becomes so much easier!

You can see that your partner or friend is trying to address something, even if not doing it very well. You can listen, ask questions, take him seriously, and respond in a way that feels good to you.

MINDFULNESS

I suggest searching on a site such as Amazon.com to find information on how to practice Mindfulness. YouTube has videos of the practice. Books, CD's, and DVD's can help you create your own practice to use daily. Making a habit of checking in on yourself physically and emotionally can allow you access to your 90/10%, and shame level when addressing conflicts.

PRACTICE NEW APPROACHES

Once you can see how you approach conflict, you can practice new responses. The best way to do this is with others who are changing their approaches, too.

I suggest finding two to five friends and making an agreement that you will study shame and conflict resolution methods together. Friends, relatives, members of 12 step meetings or attending a therapy group may be places to find like-minded people. Asking them to read these chapters could educate them about what you are looking for. Then set up regular meetings to practice exercises and watch for shame to subside.

Using your knowledgeable group, you can discover what it is like to utter critical statements. With their permission you could read the statements from the previous chapter, blasting them out with full emotion!

Notice the physical sensation in your body when you utter these critical words. Follow them with your own—those favorites that you save up for the worst times. How does that haughty, superior sensation feel? Good, doesn't it? It smashes those shameful feelings right down. It makes you feel powerful. You won't let this piece of nothing get the best of you.

You can also observe what it is like to have others act out criticism on you. Invite others to say the shaming sentences when looking right at you.

NON VIOLENT COMMUNICATION

I would like to recommend *Nonviolent Communication: A Language of Life*, by Marshall Rosenberg. Rosenberg offers excellent ways to look at our strong emotions, and how to approach them in new ways. His thoughts can be integrated with the approaches here.

STEP BY STEP

1. Tell a group member what to say to you that will bring a defensive, shameful reaction. For example, "You never think about what I might want, do you?" Or, "That was so stupid!" Or, "You don't know how to love."

2. Dramatize your usual reactions so you can have a deeply felt experience of them. For example you could snarl back, "You just hate me, I know it. Stop talking to me! You can never say anything positive, can you? I will never do what you want, so you might as well stop asking!" When your group can laugh together then it is time to try more new ways!

94

3. What would you would say if you had no shame, if you didn't feel criticized?

Looking your group member right in the eyes, see if you can experience a *reaching out sensation in your chest and arms.*

"Did you want something that I didn't see? I'd like to know about it."

"I'm sorry you feel that way, I tried to think about you."

"That feels really hurtful. If there is something specific you are thinking of, I'd like to know, but being called thoughtless feels bad."

"Can you say that differently? I can't hear you when you push me away like that."

"I'm sliding into my Avoidant style. I'm freezing up, and I can't think clearly. I may have to take a break and talk more later."

"I'm feeling hurt. Wow. My tears want to come."

If you communicate the feeling itself instead of criticisms, you might say the following sentences:

•When you ordered the take-out you wanted and didn't ask if I wanted something too, it hurt my feelings.

•When you leave a mess in the bedroom and bathroom, I have to clean it up, and this doesn't feel fair. I'd like you to clean up after yourself.

•What you just said isn't true. I really don't like it when you lie or distort things. Then I can't trust you.

•What can we do about these things that we have clearly said are not appropriate? I'm upset again, and I need a solution.

•What goes on when you make decisions like that? Are you mad at me or something? That wasn't good thinking.

•When you do these same harmful things over and over I wonder if I should leave. Please know that it is hurtful to me, and I can't continue being hurt.

Notice that even these statements can be said with open questioning, or with shaming, critical tones. See if you can imagine leaning forward, making eye contact, focused on really communicating. This is in contrast to encountering criticism and the other styles which are blasted out with no comprehension of how they affect someone else.

It helps to practice with people you are not close to, and who aren't actually critical, because your shame won't be as triggered. As you come to see that negative methods of resolving conflict really fail, and that shame is your obstacle, you can claim the freedom to practice with your future partner.

4. Try different language. Try describing how you want to shame him instead of doing it.

"I am so angry with you, I want to put you down. I want you to be quiet and get away from me. I just hate it when you tell me I should have done something I didn't."

"When I'm feeling anxious I need to direct some negativity at you. You react so predictably, although it makes me feel bad later. Then I have to be loving to get you to forgive me."

Or find out what is going on for you. Start with knowing that even if your partner has done something really objectionable, condemning him doesn't accomplish anything. It is false power. Once you can see the hopelessness of the usual approach, think about what you might say instead. What would communicate your feelings, and *reach out* toward your partner, instead of *pushing her or him away*. What would healthy anger look like?

5. Set up a regular time with others to do exercises. This can facilitate carrying through. We have found groups to be highly beneficial because it can help to watch other people practice, too.

When meeting regularly to do this,
we create a new sub-culture in which
healthy methods become standard.

This offsets the effect of our culture where harmful methods are standard! Where shaming is normal!

6. Next, try an exercise in private with just your partner or your date. If you aren't with anyone, ask a close friend or someone with whom you would like to have better conflict skills. Notice that this is more difficult without group support.

Work slowly, breathe, and stop any time
the emotions are too uncomfortable.

7. Here is the big one. Try an actual argument. One of you will know of a conflict that hasn't been resolved. Bring it up. Sit across from each other. One person names the conflict. Then take turns saying what

you *feel* when addressing it. What are the *emotions*, not the *thoughts* about it.

8. The real test will be when conflicts surface by themselves. Something new will come up that you didn't know was in waiting, something you don't agree on, that you will need to resolve. Whoever recognizes it first can say, "Okay, here is our test! We have something to talk about. Let's sit across from each other and see what we can do!" Then, slowly, begin talking. Slowly, observe your desire to use the old style. Just as slowly, change the words in your head before they come out of your mouth. Then, slowly, say the words. Wait to see how they are received.

STONEWALLING

Stonewalling is silent, and requires a different approach. In your practice group, assume the role of the stonewaller, and then take the position of the one who is trying to talk with the stonewaller. Notice how it feels to push someone away with silence. Then notice how it feels when the other person ignores you, acts as if you aren't there, and goes about their activities, now literally *out of the relationship*.

If you use stonewalling during conflict, you will now get to experience what it is like to be entirely eliminated from relating. Not only is it very painful, but it does nothing to lead to the next step. Perhaps there is no next step until both of you become calm and think more clearly, but taking a break this way is harmful to your partner. Better to yell that you are taking a break and going out or upstairs than withdraw into yourself and stop existing to your partner.

When you find that you are using mostly new conflict resolution styles, you get to jump up and down and cheer yourselves! You did it!

Chapter 13

Discovering Your Attachment Style

We have now covered the five central areas involved in creating new love. These are:

1. Relationship shame
2. Conflict resolution
3. Attachment style
4, Sexual glue
5. Projections of the past onto the present

Now let's return to this critical arena of attachment styles. The love attachment includes all of the other areas, too. *Sexual glue* creates it, *conflict res*olution styles either enhance or destroy it, *shame* interferes with conflict resolution, and our attachment history creates our *projections* onto others.

So let's take a look at how you can name your own style in order to discover a foundation for creating new love.

FIND YOUR STYLE

Taking a look at how you form attachments with your primary partners, and how you approach life in general, can help you avoid conflicts with a potential friend or partner. As I have made clear, Anxious Attachers and Avoidant Attachers will have difficulty when together. As the Anxious wants more, the Avoider will pull away. As the Avoider pulls away, the Anxious wants more. And around and around.

When you are ready for a mate, the first step is assessing your and the other person's style. This can be done by talking and talking about your preferences. If he wants to sleep every night in his own bed, alone, in his own house, will that be acceptable? If you like lots of time alone, perhaps it will be. But if your ideal is sleeping together every night in the same house, it won't. If you go forward, even with excellent conflict resolution skills, the *conflicts will not be resolvable.*

Once you enter a relationship the time has come to *communicate* about attachment needs. The secret to successful relating lies in being able to *tell the other person what you are thinking and feeling.* If you just say "I'm feeling distant," or "I want to be alone," or "I can't talk anymore," the other person could take this to mean something about your feelings toward him or her. If you can address these needs by saying, "My Avoidant is showing up," you will be owning that this is an issue of yours. If you and your partner have had previous discussions about it, she will understand. She may still react because she wants you close, but her reaction will be more about the present instead of based on insecurities or her own past. *She is more likely to stay in the 10% instead of going to the 90% history.*

If you are Anxious, and feeling dependent, frightened, and needy, your partner might be driven away in self-defense. But if you can say that you are in your Anxious Attachment, he will more easily step back and assess what to do. Knowing that this is a style, he may take it less personally, and then not feel obligated to sacrifice for you, or to leave. On the contrary, he may actually step forward and give you reassurance. If you can openly express what you need, he may be able to take care of you!

Understanding these styles is vital in order to protect a new relationship. Think about what is true for you. Here is more detail.

SECURE ATTACHMENT

The Secure Attachment is that well functioning state in which we are

> *balanced between a sense of oneness with our mate*
> *and the independence of our own life.*

Both people are able to assess what is best for each, and for the relationship. There is no need to compromise since there is no sacrifice. Being in relationship is congruent with the independent living of one's own life. Securely Attached people are able to access the instinctive knowing of how relationships work. They have not lived according to the culture's norms. We can assume they had Secure Attachments with their mothers, and did not have to abandon their instinctive knowing. They had little shame to handle.

I believe that marriages by such people are rare. Thus, the high divorce rate, and the many unhappy marriages that don't end.

ANXIOUS ATTACHMENT

The Anxiously Attached person focuses on the partner with a great deal of energy, attention, sacrifice, criticism, fear, and other clingy, needy responses. Those who are Anxiously Attached, or who are in relationship with someone who is, have the task of differentiating between natural reactions to a relationship in potential trouble (10%) and a history of fear in relating to important others (90%).

The child who discovered that when she whined and cried, she got Mother to respond with at least some attention, might very well whine and cry with her mate. She may figure out how to get him to feel guilty or responsible so that he will give her some kind of attention. She may perceive her need as real and his response as really needed, even though they aren't needed in the 10% present. Both she and her partner can learn how to reassure her in order to heal the past. However, it will fail if they set out to re-do the history:

He cannot give her enough attention to make up for her childhood deprivation.

Below are examples of the behaviors of the Anxiously Attached. However, before I begin the list, I need to caution you that these reactions are also triggered in those with Secure Attachment when threatened by a partner's Avoidant behavior, narcissism, or controlling style. These are the natural emotions that I recount in Chapter 2. You may need to ask for help in differentiating which of your reactions are from Anxious Attachment, which are natural to falling in love, and which are reactions to abusive behavior. How you address each one is, of course, different.

• Excessive monitoring of or obsession with the partner's behavior, thoughts, and feelings.
• Strong reactions to slight infractions.

•Putting your needs second to hers.

•Repeatedly feeling deeply hurt.

•Criticizing, condemning, and tantrum throwing in reaction to partner's behavior.

•Irrational fear of loss of partner through affairs, abandonment, or death.

•Believing you cannot live without your partner.

AVOIDANT ATTACHMENT

Avoidant maneuvers are *unconscious*. They are a form of dissociation from the actual experience of present life in order to avoid feeling bad. *Reacting like that is not something that we simply decide to do.* We must appreciate this so that we don't expect ourselves or our partners to just decide to stop. What we can do is learn to recognize when we or our partners go into Avoidant maneuvers. Then we can name them, and perhaps stop them.

As an Avoidant Attacher most of my life, I couldn't see my 90% because it worked well. I effectively had no fear, I moved on when things didn't go well, I was enviably boundaried. I was able to lead an unusual life. As a young mother in a neighborhood of housewives raising their children, I went off to graduate school and then opened a therapy practice. Change went well and was welcome. I looked good. I didn't know that

*the empty feeling that pervaded my life was from
not attaching in the ways that we are naturally intended.*

It was disconcerting to even consider dropping my style of sending people away or leaving. When the phrases, "get the fuck out," and "I'm out of here," ran through my mind, I could finally use them to alert me that I was trying to shift into a place of seeming safety. I had to practice saying, instead, "I'm having that desire to be done—to leave, or to send you away. But it's just my Avoider. It's not real."

I had to discover the difference between ending and just having emotional boundaries. When things really aren't going to go forward in an argument, it can be useful for both people to separate for minutes or hours. Coming together after things settle down can allow processing to go more smoothly. The voices from the past can still play in your mind, but you are just trying to use old methods of feeling better. Or, rather, not feeling badly. Hurt, anger, betrayal, and loss can all be set aside when you walk away! But they are only set aside, they are not gone. It's better to become able to handle hurt, anger, betrayal and loss.

Here are some ways people Avoidantly Attach. The full list is endless.

•Preferring silence, staying in one's own thoughts.
•Looking at people's clothing, body shapes, and other sources of evaluation.
•Shopping for unnecessary items, for the sake of it.
•Changing the subject in conversation.
•Dominating conversation in a small group while having no connection to the others.
•Going off by yourself when company is visiting.
•Having a strong desire to end a relationship over a small conflict.
•Using alcohol or drugs to change moods, and provide a predictable outcome.
•Over-focusing on work or projects, feeling consumed so that relationships become secondary.
•Flirting with others to dilute the attachment
•Having affairs to dilute attachment.
•Using porn and or fantasy to be sexual with mate, or without the mate.
•Looking at nature, appreciating beauty, in order to pull away.
•Preferring a lot of sex as a form of yearning for connection.
•Preferring little or no sex in order to avoid too much intimacy.
•Spending a good deal of time in fantasy – sexual, work, creative projects, etc.
•Having solitary hobbies.

The book, *Attached,* by Levine provides examples that will help you recognize your style. Just as important, it will help you perceive the styles of those you date and those you wish to partner with.

AMBIVALENT ATTACHMENT

People who don't attach well still yearn to do so! We all want to love and be loved, and when this need is thwarted, it becomes intense. We miss it.

Thus appears the Ambivalent form of Attachment style. A person may vacillate between Avoidant and Anxious, or even express both at the same time.

Men who abuse their partners, who criticize and condemn, will finally reach the end of their need to avoid. They have at last satisfied the need to either push their partners away or to pull away themselves. But once distant, then yearning for what they truly need arises. They may cry and apologize, promising to never do it again. Clients ask which is accurate – the push away or the pulling closer. Both are true. *Going to one extreme breeds going to the other*.

I had one date with a man who swung to both extremes. When I saw that he wasn't a candidate for a relationship, I offered to be friends with no possibility of anything more. At our second meeting he was nervous. He said that I came on strong, asking lots of questions, when in my mind I was just being friendly and interested in getting acquainted. When he could tell me what he was feeling, I reassured him that I truly wanted only friendship. But once he could see that I wasn't after him, he focused intently on me. I had to struggle to get in my car to leave. He asked for a hug, and as I responded, he tried to kiss me.

The fear that led him to avoid attaching was as strong as the clinging that expressed his Anxious Attachment. I wondered what it had been like for those women who had lasted a year with him.

AVOIDANT

Most of those who are single late in life have had difficulty entering or remaining in relationship. The workaholic, the mother who focuses more on her children, the person who is afraid of engaging intimately with others may use Avoidant maneuvers to feel emotionally safe.

I found that most of the men I encountered on Internet dating sites were Avoidant Attachers. They wrote profiles expressing their ability to be honest, communicate well, and love someone forever. But in conversation they talked non-stop, with no interest in who I was or what I might want to talk about. Each acted the part of an interesting man with interesting things to say, but had no perception of me. They were unable to interact openly, warmly, and with genuine interest. Avoidant Attachment can prevent empathy. This is a real loss for each of these men, and of course for their partners. I sadly turned each away. I couldn't explain this with enough compassion to prevent them from feeling shame. Some clearly felt bad. Others criticized me so that they didn't have to feel shame. Rejection is difficult.

HOW TO HANDLE AVOIDANT STYLES

Attached: The New Science of Adult Attachment offers a starter list of ways that create distance from partners. However, people don't usually know that their need for distance is because of an attachment style. Instead they come up with explanations that seem to make logical sense.

You need to understand your and your partner's style of pushing each other away. Once you can *see* it, you have a chance of *naming* it, and then using better ways to create separation.

DISTANCING MECHANISMS DESCRIBED IN *ATTACHED*.

•Even while staying together, saying you aren't ready to commit.
•Focusing on small imperfections and believing they mean this person isn't right for you.
•Fantasizing about an ex-lover.
•Searching for the perfect lover.
•Flirting with others.
•Not being able to say, "I love you."
•Pulling away when things are going well.
•Choosing someone with no future, i.e., someone who is married.
•Checking out mentally when the partner is talking.
•Secret-keeping and leaving things foggy in order to feel independent.
•Avoiding physical closeness – not sleeping in the same bed, walking ahead of partner, not wanting sex.

I added the following:

•Starting fights for no reason.
•Criticizing your partner for things about which he or she is sensitive.
•Turning to an addictive substance or behavior.
•Leading parallel lives with little intimate exchange.
•Becoming silent and withdrawn when feeling hurt or misunderstood.

IDENTIFYING ATTACHMENT BEHAVIORS: MAKING A LIST

Once you have an idea of the choices, get together with friends or your group, and talk about your behaviors that you think qualify for the different styles. Ask them to reflect back to you the accuracy of your perceptions, or if they see you otherwise. I find it useful to make a list, as it is easy to believe that attachment behaviors are just rational ways to behave! As we learn to recognize our behaviors as attachment defenses, then we have the chance to observe ourselves and invite change.

Chapter 14

Changing Attachment Behaviors While Honoring Your Style

We have developed a style from early childhood based on how our parents related to us. We can use this information to create a more secure relationship. As we examine emotions and attitudes coming from the 90% history, we can ask what our attachment with our mothers and other important attachment figures may have been like. From that examination, we can more easily guess how we are projecting that onto the present and onto our partner.

NAMING YOUR ATTACHMENT BEHAVIORS

Wouldn't it be nice if we could learn how we create distance, or how we try to pull our partners in close against their will, and then magically change? Perhaps some behaviors can be easily changed, but our basic approach to feeling safe will change slowly. However,

> *if we can discover what we automatically do*
> *when uncomfortable,*
> *and tell our partner all about it,*
> *we can offset some of the conflicts that arise.*

If your partner knows that you will become anxious, or you will pull away, he will be less triggered into thinking that he will be drained of life, or that it is over. Reading *Attached* together can provide an education about how it all works, so you can understand yourselves, and each other, better.

We are programmed to feel discomfort when our partner pulls away, but if we know it's just his style of feeling safe, and that he can't help it, we stand a better chance of not fearing abandonment.

If she exhibits strong fear, pulls on you, asks for touch and time, you may need appropriate boundaries. But you can understand, too, that she may be comforted by some attention, and that she isn't trying to suck your energy dry. (Well, unless her needs are extreme, and then that is the eventual outcome.)

As with conflict resolution, the first step is always *observing*. Learn about your style by paying attention to it. Ask friends to observe together. Join a group in which everyone educates everyone else about how their style manifests. These maneuvers are so much easier to observe in others first, before extending the new understanding to ourselves. Do you know what it's like when you begin practicing a new skill—perhaps in a work setting or in school—and all of a sudden you realize that you know what you're doing? That's how this works.

We will take a look at the effect of two people with different attachment styles joining together in a partnership. If we understand ours and theirs, we stand a better chance of picking someone with whom we can be compatible.

AVOIDANT WITH AVOIDANT

Ruth liked to come home from work, take a half hour for herself before beginning dinner, cook by herself, eat, and then watch TV until going to bed with the TV on. Her husband felt rejected, unloved, unwanted, and alone. When he brought up his displeasure, Ruth told him that this was her way of life and it wouldn't change. He grew more distant himself, finally had an affair, and left her.

After the divorce when she began dating, Ruth realized that she needed to talk about her lifestyle on every first date. She figured that if a man would have difficulty with her isolated style, as her ex husband had, she might as well find out right away. She did. Most men said no thanks, and moved on. But finally she found a man who liked to work in the garage, work in the yard, and watch TV when in the house! What a match!

When Ruth and her new love went out to dinner, and practiced checking in with what they were feeling, both named that they were comfortable with only one hour of conversation. This was their limit.

Both liked to have the other in the house, though. As they learned to talk about their feelings, they discovered what each needed and wanted. It was easy as long as they didn't have to interact. They planned weekend activities that focused on reading and getting things done.

Sex provided glue, even though their eyes were closed most of the time. As you might imagine, they didn't talk!. Both knew they were loved and accepted even though they didn't express their emotions. Either of them could have interpreted the other's behavior as rejecting, but since they could name what was going on, they could identify each other's style.

This marriage was a perfect example of finding someone who matches your style. However, if they hadn't talked about it, either could have felt rejected or unwanted in the face of the partner's behavior.

ANXIOUS WITH ANXIOUS

Jenny and Jack were both Anxious Attachers. When Jenny dated, she was always afraid the man wouldn't like her, and she tried to present herself well. When the man didn't, she was devastated even if he wasn't interesting to her. When she met Jack she had already learned that if she named her fears as symptoms, she might encounter someone who understood. Jack's Anxious Attachment emotions didn't begin until a second or third date, when it looked as if things might move forward. Then his fear emerged, and he had difficulty carrying on comfortable conversation.

They met for coffee one Saturday morning, and Jenny started right out telling Jack that she was afraid and that the anxiety was interfering with her ability to talk easily. Jack was amazed. He had never encountered more than: What do you like to do, where do you work, and how many children do you have! He started to laugh as he told her that he had the same fear, but his didn't show up right away. They agreed that they would tell each other any time they were afraid. By the end of their first dinner they agreed that if they observed the other becoming awkward or stilted they would ask if he or she was feeling fear. It can often be easier to see someone else's fear before one's own.

By the time they added sexual glue they were well practiced in saying when they were afraid. They could actually laugh over their statements of fear. It was the first time neither had to worry about performing, doing it right, looking right, and otherwise being what the other person wanted. They just focused on feeling their fear.

Becoming able to name the awful experience of fear allowed them to name other feelings, too. As they received reassurance that they were loved, and the other wasn't leaving, they both became Securely Attached. Anxiously Attached people are capable of creating a Secure Attachment when they can name their emotions, and when they can take them into account. They can

create a healthy dependency that actually
allows each to feel stronger and more independent.

AVOIDANT WITH ANXIOUS

Ruth's first marriage is an example of how difficult it is when one person is very Avoidant and the other isn't. Her husband was capable of Secure Attachment, and wanted a more "normal" marriage in which they related more. Communication could not correct this. One of them would have to change their attachment style in order for the marriage to meet the needs of both.

When a strong Avoidant couples with an Anxious Attacher, the relationship just may not work. This is a reason to go slowly when getting to know someone. Avoidants may not look Avoidant when they are first falling in love because initially, they are pulled into affection and romance in ways they may not be able to maintain. Many people pull away as time goes on.

If a couple decides to go forward, it will help to
discover each one's style and describe it to the other.

If you try to avoid rejection by presenting yourself in false ways, you set yourself up for great disappointment and pain – and then rejection.

Imagine that first date. One kind of Avoidant is reserved and friendly, but self contained. She checks to see what the other person is like, and has no pre-determined need or assumptions. She is willing to dismiss the other person over any indication that he wouldn't be of interest.

The Anxious is very different. He is sweating, wondering if he has chosen the right clothing, and afraid that he won't know what to say. He smiles awkwardly, hoping for an indication that he is welcomed. Opposites!

We can guess the course of this date. The Avoidant immediately feels done, while the Anxious is still hoping. Their conversation would be awkward unless the Avoidant talks non-stop and relieves the Anxious of the demand.

But if they had read this book, assessed their own style, and knew the resulting behaviors and emotions, it might have gone differently. The Avoidant could say, You seem to be an Anxious, is this right? Anxious could say Yes, and feel relief on having it out in the open. If Avoidant has any interest in him, she could smile and give reassurance with a touch on the arm, or saying something like, "Let's just talk for a while and see what happens." As Anxious names his discomfort he is likely to feel less of it, and more able to come forward.

These two may still not be a match, but they will have created the opportunity to find out. If they go forward they will know in advance that each will have to take the other's style into consideration. Anxious will know that Avoidant will not be available in ways he may want. Avoidant will know that she will need to reassure Anxious in a way that she, herself, doesn't need.

The beginning will be smoother
than if they expected
the other to be like themselves

AVOIDANT WITH SOMEWHAT ANXIOUS

Hudson was an Avoidant Attacher who fell in love with a woman who was somewhat Anxious. He had compartments in his life that he didn't invite her into. He believed that secrets and deceptions were normal and acceptable, even necessary. His style developed when growing up in a family where emotional isolation was needed in order to maintain a semblance of his individuality. He feared turning his personality over to his partner and abandoning his true sense of self. He hung onto this true sense by hiding those compartments in which he could be himself.

Olivia felt bereft over the absence of a Secure Attachment. She expressed hurt and chagrin as she discovered his compartments. When she confronted him about lies and other deceptions, he felt no remorse and gave no apology. Her hurt didn't register as a reason for him to change.

Hudson's Avoidant Attachment style allowed him a deep experience of individuality. He was not willing to let this go. Since he had difficulty understanding the need he was trying to meet, he couldn't understand the nature of a Securely Attached relationship. Instead, he wanted to create a list of rules that both would follow. This contract was to make them *feel* secure. The agreements included sexual monogamy, spending regular time together, doing what you say you are going to do, and taking a superficial interest in each other's lives. They engaged in predictable activities and could count on each other.

But without understanding the Securely Attached relationship, Hudson couldn't understand why Olivia wanted more. He was unable to name his Avoidant maneuvers, or even to understand that he was avoiding something.

Olivia tried to explain, gave him books to read, and cried with each betrayal. She finally left. He was unable to grasp why one more woman walked away.

Olivia had assumed that any man wanted what she did. After this marriage, she decided to ask any potential lover to read this book and work together to identify what they were looking for. When she read about Secure Attachments, she could see that this is what she had expected, only to find that many people did not want the same. Perhaps it's more accurate to say that

> *some people's ways of protecting their sense of self*
> *forbids a deeply attached love relationship.*

They believe they must remain superficial in order to remain emotionally safe.

Ruth and her second husband did not keep themselves out of each other's lives. So they were compatible. But Hudson's need to live in isolation while appearing to be in relationship doesn't work for a partner wanting a real relationship. Perhaps he can find someone who will match him if he knows what to ask in that first meeting. He could explain that he doesn't break the law or have affairs, but he has activities and friendships that he doesn't want to talk about. If he meets someone who feels the same, they will be on the same page. However, both will feel deprived, too. Our instincts compel us to want a Secure Attachment.

The sad truth for Avoidants is that we all want love. Even the most extreme Avoidant wants to look into a partner's eyes, see love, and feel his love is received. But it will frighten him. He created this attachment style when he was very small for a good reason, and it feels essential to life now. If he can't enter a healing process to understand what he is trying to do, and how it now fails, he is stuck with trying to meet a perceived need for safety.

People like Hudson can heal from their attachment history of deprivation or abuse, but they must be motivated to go to therapy and examine those old pains. He would have to learn who he really is, how he wants to live his life, and be able to communicate that to a partner. He will have to give up thinking relationships include sacrifice and rules of conduct, and replace them with boundaries that come with really knowing himself. Some people take on this task and find the process very rewarding. But others cannot perceive that there is a need or understand the process of meeting it.

BECOMING SEEMINGLY ANXIOUS

All people can look like Anxious Attachers once they fall in love. If the partner seems unavailable or removed – Avoidant – it can trigger those natural human emotions of fear, hurt, and betrayal. These emotions so woven into love relationships are easily provoked, and then they look like Anxious Attachment.

A friend dated three different men over several years. The first worked long hours, ran marathons, and had little time for dating. She felt threatened all the time and obsessed over his lack of commitment. Finally he stopped calling. He probably couldn't handle the pressure of her need. She appeared to be an Anxious Attacher.

Her second lover was more attentive, took her to interesting places and was romantic. After the honeymoon period, she again felt bereft, as if something important was missing. Again I told her she was an Anxious Attacher.

But her new love doesn't trigger such behavior. A year and a half later, he calls her every day. He tells her all about his busy life. He wants to know about hers. He listens to her. They see each once or twice a week, yet she does not worry that he isn't really interested in her! He doesn't trigger that seemingly Anxious emotion. His Secure Attachment approach allows her to feel connected even though he actually has less time to be with her than the other two men had. The difference is that she knows exactly why. She knows where he is and hears all about it afterwards. He shares his troubles with his work and about his ex. He is real with her.

*When Avoidant and Anxious people become able to
tell each other what is going on with them,
they create intimacy.*

This is true even when it means saying they need space, need to be alone, need to focus elsewhere! Transparency about one's life makes the other feel safe. When we feel safe we get that wonderful experience of *independence*! Strong feelings of dependence are triggered when the other person pulls away in order to lead his own separate life. Then we *look like* Anxious Attachers.

CHANGING ATTACHMENT BEHAVIORS

The examples above show that we don't necessarily have to change our Attachment style in order to make a partnership work. While that would help, we can protect our relationship by coming to *understand* our style, and *describing* it to our partner. This can help create a well-working, safe relationship.

THE IMPACT OF SHAME

There are many people around us who are unable to offer transparency to their partner. Those who break the law, cheat others in business, cheat sexually, or behave any other shame-producing way will not be able to fully reveal themselves to their mate. When *a secret is held off to the side*, whether it's a lover or a DUI, it prevents the fullest experience of a Securely Attached relationship.

Those who engage in illegal, unethical, or just unacceptable practices must hide these in compartments where they can't be seen. Partners sense this even if they have no concrete information. Have you had that experience of finally learning that something you have vaguely suspected is in fact true? Followed by a profound sense of having known but not believed it? This vague sense will prevent feeling safe in the relationship because safety comes from knowing that you are truly connected in all ways with your mate. Secrets prevent this.

Everyone feels shame for something they have done, are doing, or are thinking. Confronting these behaviors and relieving the shame will assist you in creating the most intimate relationship. Just telling someone about it can reduce shame. (Unless, of course, your partner will shame you for it.)

Chapter 15

Enhancing Relationship Glue

In this chapter we will look at how to pull yourself into the bond, how to use sex to enhance relating, enhance love, and support a Secure Attachment. In the next chapter we will look at how we are pulled away from the sexual bond.

It is generally assumed that when a couple starts dating they will kiss as a communication of more than mild interest and will move on at some point to having sex. But little attention is given by the media and in conversation to how this might unfold in ways that *enhance the attachment*. Below are suggestions that may help a couple in the early stages of falling in love.

TALKING

While the need to talk about sex seems obvious, in the same way that people talk about who's cooking and who's doing the dishes, couples don't do it! This is because of the layers and layers of shame that overlay this part of our humanity. The exception is when talking about sex in an arousing manner, as couples do in phone sex.

Arousal, being a very good drug,
prevents the shame from being felt.

When dating, if you and your partner think that you may very well move toward sex, it's time to start talking. Express an interest, and find out if he or she has one as well.

Don't use kissing as the communication.

Let yourself be aware of and feel any discomfort, and tell her. Laugh together about how hard it can be to talk about this. Discuss the path you might take. Lying down together, only kissing at first. How are the clothes taken off? In the dark? Daylight? Do they only come off if full sexual activity is agreed upon?

Talk about what you like to do, what is arousing, what limits you might have. Talk about erections. Men worry about not getting them. Their partners have reactions when they don't, often questioning their attractiveness, fearing that he is not interested after all. These possible difficulties can be handled by conversation across a table or on the phone. You don't want him to create and keep an erection to the exclusion of being present with you.

When performing *sexually,*
couples are not exchanging relationship glue

TAKING IT SLOWLY

The sexual glue is so powerful that it is best to introduce it slowly. Our culture has made it okay to have sex within the first few dates, but this will bond you into a couple when you may not be right for each other. It has brought heartache for many when they have to grieve away the bond after one or the other realizes the relationship isn't right, or when they stay with the wrong person for a long time, or for life.

When a couple attends to their conflict resolution styles, attachment behaviors, and sexuality before introducing the glue, they will be better prepared for the powerful connection it creates. Of course just being interested in each other brings some of this glue.

Talk first. Act later. Take weeks, even months, to truly get to know each other.

ATTACHMENT STYLE AND GLUE

When two people are exploring the decision to become a couple, learning about each of their attachment styles will help them understand their own and each other's sexuality.

For example, Avoidant Attachers who cannot communicate their emotions well may find sex to be more important to them than it is to others. They feel a need for closeness that doesn't require talking about themselves. Or they may need the intensity of sex to open themselves to being with someone.

I had two dates with a man who wanted to engage sexually right away. Upset when I told him it had to wait, he explained that sex would bring falling in love more quickly than conversation. Then once we fell in love, conflicts and issues would become meaningless and the relationship would work. *He wanted to use sexual glue to override problems.*

One danger of using sex for this purpose is that if the partner doesn't feel the need for the same frequency, a common relationship issue emerges. This is when one person frequently asks for sex, the second says no, the first feels hurt and unloved, the second feels pressured and gives in to a certain frequency. But the first person still doesn't feel loved because the sex isn't love-making, it's duty. It's servicing. Complaints about this disparity appear frequently in therapists' offices.

Some Avoidant Attachers cannot have intimate sex. They are limited by their need to avoid deeply felt love, so sex must be relegated to physically good feelings. It is seen as a need to be fulfilled, and an obligation of both people. While this use of sex may be enjoyable, and possibly acceptable to both, it is far from full out relationship glue. I have met with couples who said their sex life was great, but they didn't love each other and wanted to divorce!

WHEN SEX HAS "MEANING"

When sex is used to prove something it no longer glues the couple into an intimate, loving bond. Lovemaking cannot verify that you are sexy, attractive, loved, valued, or permanent. The phrase, "good in bed," is a drastic misplacement of the function of sex. When people are not connected, when they are engaged in sex for some meaning other than creating a relationship, they will not have full access to their experience of themselves or each other.

Those who have sufficiently reduced their sexual shame and are in touch with their loving feelings will *discover* what pleases both. This is an inside-out sexual interaction that is not based on "doing it right." But cultural shaming of sex has resulted in this natural approach having to be learned.

Glue comes from wanting to be a couple.

Then the arousal, looking into each other's eyes, and melting into a sense of oneness brings you even closer. Examining your interpretations of the meaning of sex can help you remove them so that you can glue lovingly.

EMOTIONS AFTER INTRODUCING SEX

Avoidant Attachers may allow sex to glue them to their mate and then feel uncomfortable later. In their need to return to their sense of separateness, they might pull away. They can roll over after sex, fall asleep, not want to be around the partner the next day, start fights, or otherwise create distance.

If both people are Avoidant this may work. But if one is Secure or Anxious this is going to provoke distress if it isn't understood. However, if you know your partner is going to pull away after closeness because of his or her defensive style, and you don't take it personally, it might be tolerated.

When the Avoidant needs to go to great lengths to pull away and maintain separation, he or she may find the partner unattractive, upsetting, or demanding, or may focus on small details that are found to be objectionable.

Anxious Attachers may cling to the partner, over-emphasizing the effect of the glue. They may assume that the relationship is more bonded than it is, imagine the wedding, and expect all of the Securely Attached behaviors to immediately appear.

Understandably, the Secure Attacher or the Avoidant will react to the anxiety of the Anxious Attacher, and want to pull back. Providing reassurance to the insecure person, and explaining one's need to create distance can minimize the hurt.

Chapter 16

Preserving Relationship Glue

THE ROLE OF JEALOUSY

As long as there is no sexual infidelity, our culture sees jealousy as an issue for the one who feels it, instead of taking a look at subtle violations of the relationship. Below are examples in which *the jealous partner reflects natural emotions coming from the desire for a Securely Attached love relationship.* If you have experienced one or more of these please remember that they are culturally acceptable. You are not alone.

•Conflict: Charles' wife, Jean, has a friendship with her ex. They worked together to remodel her home, they went out to dinner a couple of times a month, and they talked regularly on the phone. Neither felt anything sexual for the other, but their history made them closer than if they had met as just friends.

Charles had a problem with Jean's feelings for her ex and wanted her to stop relating with him. Jean understood that even though there is nothing sexual involved, her new love would not want to have the sensation of knowing she is with someone she used to love, have sex with, sleep with, and live with. That old attachment made Charles uncomfortable. He and Jean had a conflict to resolve.

Resolution: Jean had difficulty understanding Charles's discomfort until she met an ex of Charles'. He set this up in order to ask her how she would feel if the tables were turned. Even though he actually didn't care for his ex, Jean realized that she wouldn't like to hear about dinners and projects they shared if he were to do what she did. And so she lovingly stopped her relationship with her ex. She understood that a history of living together, sleeping together, and engaging sexually made the present relationship different than friendship.

Some couples are able to integrate old lovers into the new relationship. Some are not.

118

•Lisa walked into a club where she was going to meet her fiancé at some point in the evening. She saw him sitting at the bar talking with a woman. As she walked toward them, the woman reached out and touched his arm, smiling seductively. Her husband didn't flirt back.

Conflict: Lisa was upset because he didn't leave the woman or tell her that he wasn't available. Eventually he understood that letting someone flirt with him was deceptive to the woman and violated the deep monogamous bond he felt with Lisa.

Resolution: Her upset disappeared when he lovingly told her he would set limits in the future. He had liked the small hit from being seen as attractive and interesting by a sexy woman. Once he could see that this wasn't something real when he was with a stranger, and was attention that belonged in his marriage, he *wanted* to stop. He later enjoyed telling a flirtatious woman to please not flirt with him since he wasn't available.

•Conflict: John liked to look at women he found attractive. His wife told him that she was hurt when she saw his head turn while they were in the middle of a conversation.

Resolution: He realized that scanning for someone to look at was a small violation of his sexuality. He knew that if his wife scanned for attractive men, he would feel as if he weren't enough. He wouldn't feel safe. Not that he expected his wife to leave him for one of them—it was having a sense of being safely bonded, and deeply attached.

•I described Hudson's Avoidant compartments earlier, and we can now see how this would trigger jealousy.

Conflict: Hudson walked away from his partner toward a server in a restaurant, talked with her about the sunset they were watching, and described the one he had seen the night before. His lover stood 30 feet away, left out, noticing that he didn't say that they had watched the sunset together the night before. Even if this had been a friend she would have felt left out. But this was the man she loved talking flirtatiously with an attractive woman as if she weren't in the room.

The Glue began evaporating.

No resolution: Hudson could not understand his lover's emotional reaction because he didn't know that he was actually motivated by a passive aggression. He had succeeded in making her pay for an insult he had experienced earlier. He wasn't able to see that he had caused hurt and then repair the damage.

•Patti smiled as she enjoyed the aftermath of lovemaking until her man began talking about how a past lover was capable of intense orgasms, and how he had helped her have them. Knowing that he was thinking of sex with someone else felt stabbing. The closeness changed to distance.

•A friend told me about when he was having intercourse with his wife, she started talking about the people they had met that evening. He was hurt when he realized that she was merely allowing him to relieve himself, that they weren't making love.

The Glue didn't bind them well any longer.

•The culture says that porn is not a healthy use of sexuality, yet more than half of Americans use it on a regular basis. There is no reason for shame for this, but you might take a look at how it *softens relationship glue*. If you want all of your sexual energy to be exchanged only with your lover, you will have to let this go. If Avoidantly Attached, you may decide to not give it up. Some of the relationship safety can be maintained by discussing this with your partner so that you don't keep secrets.

Roberta walked into the home office to find her husband masturbating to porn on the computer. She knew that he masturbated, but didn't know that he looked at pictures of other women. At first he talked about how lots of men did this, but as she expressed hurt about the infidelity he came to see that even though he wasn't having sex with anyone, he was relating sexually with people other than her.

•Secrets prevent good glue connection, too. When Jim started seeing Mary he didn't want to tell her that he still saw his old girlfriend. They weren't sexual, and he knew there was no future there, but he didn't want Mary to know. When she accidentally found evidence, he felt caught and guilty. He realized that if he kept secrets like this that Mary couldn't trust him. So he began answering her questions about parts of his life that he hadn't disclosed. He worked hard to become worthy of her trust. As he relaxed into openness, he became more emotionally available to Mary. Her trust evolved from his words and from his very attitude of openness. Their glue expanded, pulling them warmly together. Jim was grateful that he had been "caught."

120

•When Jackie and Rob went to parties, Jackie swept into the room looking for people she knew, talking even with those she didn't. Rob knew this was how she was, but he always felt as if he stopped existing in her mind when others were around. When he brought this up, she felt controlled, saying she didn't want him hovering around waiting for attention. He explained that he needed to have a sense that he was still her foundation before he could enjoy her talking with others.

After several fights she finally realized that she did, indeed, leave him behind. At the next party she held onto his hand when talking with others. This kept her attention on him—on them, actually. She found she could do this without abandoning her gregarious, extroverted delight in others. After a time he left to talk with someone else, but both felt connected in a new way. Making love later, they could *feel the glue thicken even while Rob felt more independent at events*. From then on they kept their hands together until he was ready to move away. Soon he didn't feel the need for the hand because her energy didn't leave him. They reveled in the understanding that meeting each other's need for dependence actually brought safe separation!

•Bob came up with the phrase, "spray and scan," to describe his girlfriend's attitude when she was around attractive men. She broadcasted—sprayed—sexuality with clothing, body movement and facial expressions. Then she looked around – scanning—to see who responded. He told her repeatedly that this was extremely distressing to him and asked her to stop. She said that this was who she was, that she enjoyed the attention. He came to accept this, as he had no choice if he wanted to be with her. But it prevented the warm, stretchy gooey glue from bringing them as close as possible because it prevented the fullest sense of safety—all this in spite of loving each other, having intimate sex, living together and fully sharing their lives in all other ways.

People growing up in this culture can believe that none of these acts is a violation of the relationship. I suggest that you take a look at what you do or did, and see if you can understand how your reactions prevent the deepest connection. If you are an Avoidant Attacher you may want your partner to back away from you. You may want the glue to soften, or dissolve. You may react to her hurt as if you are being scolded or shamed. You might pull away, triggering even more of her protest and upset.

If you can *talk talk talk*, you can put the relationship first, and grasp that her

> *jealousy comes from the relationship glue.*

And if she expresses her upset by criticizing and shaming you, you can ask her to

> *put it in different language.*

Chapter 17

Healing Sexual Issues

Healthy relationships make room for healthy sexuality and its gluing function. This, in turn, improves the relationship. But we live in a culture that treats sexuality badly. Lust, non-monogamy, masturbation to porn, and addictive love affairs are supported by the media. But they are not *caused* by the media. They already exist in the culture. And all of this distorts the bonding use of sex.

For example, what if a couple falls in love, moves in together, and he finds that he isn't as attracted to her as he had been. She perceives this, diets, exercises, has plastic surgery, and tries to seduce him. When that doesn't work because he is attached to porn images, she is devastated. He feels guilty, so he makes the problem about her, and tells her that she isn't attractive enough. There is nothing more she can do. They may still love each other and remain together, but the sexual issues interfere with their love.

If they set out to heal their impaired sexuality, he would discover that it is possible to remove the association of porn images from his sexual draw. He could learn that he is capable of a very different use of sex, one that supports his emotional feelings for his lover. As she is informed of his progress, she can stop feeling as if she weren't enough. She can nurture her view of herself as sexual no matter what she looks like. She can learn that

love, not body parts and lust,
could be the motivation for sex.

She can stop believing she has to be lust-worthy.

My book, *Reclaiming Healthy Sexual Energy: Revised* goes into detail about what the culture has done to our perception of sex.

SEXUAL SHAME

No one has entirely healthy sexuality!

Every single one of us has been shamed by the culture, our families, our churches, and by harmful sexual experiences.

Removing culturally supported rules about how sex should be, talking with your partner, and engaging in sexual healing can free sex to be used as the glue for the relationship.

Think about when you reached puberty and discovered an intensification of sexual feelings brought on by hormones. Were you comfortable exploring your erogenous zones? What about your first masturbation? Were you able to masturbate? Did you tell your parents about this new discovery? No?

Why is sex called dirty? Raunchy? Naughty? Why is saying what you want called "talking dirty"? Why can people tell sexual jokes, but can't talk openly about sex?

FEAR OF THE COMMITMENT GLUE

Many of you will rejoice at the idea that sex can be a glue for the unique two-person connection that makes up a couple. Some will be afraid of it at the same time. Avoidant Attachment leads some people to pull away from others, including their partner, as a way to feel emotionally safe. Some of these people will find the attachment glue to be discomfiting, and will want to deny it. They will use sex for physical pleasure only, see it only as a need that should be met, or evaluate the performance of themselves and their partners. All of this defeats the gluing effect of falling into the experience of clothes off, looking into each other's eyes, and using arousal's deeply bonding function. *Your partner may be afraid of it.*

Fear of the glue is only one reason that people use sex in non-gluing ways. Distortions of sexual views may arise from the culture, from sexual abuse, from early use of porn that anchors that perception of bodies, and from other factors. Again, my book on sexuality can show you how to remove these influences.

SEXUAL ABUSE INTERFERES WITH GLUE

A large percentage of people have been touched inappropriately during childhood, or molested outright, or received looks and comments that harmed their sexuality. These events can influence sex in adulthood, interfering with using it lovingly. Some people find a mate who can, by addressing these influences gently and lovingly, help their partner heal. Most often, however, psychotherapy is needed to truly relieve the harmful effects. Group therapy can be effective as it powerfully relieves the shame from these experiences, and shame from just living in this culture.

PORNOGRAPHY AND FANTASY DON'T SUPPORT GLUE

There is debate in the fields of sex therapy, sexual addiction recovery and incest healing about the role of pornography and fantasy. When people have difficulty becoming and staying aroused, some therapists recommend the use of porn and fantasy. Even in my own organization, the Society for the Advancement of Sexual Health (www.SASH.net), a few practitioners believe that using certain kinds of porn is not outside the healthy arena.

Some people cannot be aroused by love alone because their sexuality has been harmed. They need to use outside stimulation. This is sad, but gets to be accepted for what it is. Porn can be stimulating. Sexual fantasy can, too, and some people require it in order to achieve orgasm. If this is true for you, please don't take my comments as a reason for shame about this.

FLIRTING OR GLUE?

Some say flirting is "innocent," yet most are jealous when they see their partner flirting. True monogamy will not include flirting with others.

When all sexual energy is flooding back and forth
between two people
there isn't any left over to go elsewhere.

This may bring up discomfort for some who want separation and distance from time to time. The irony is that the stronger the glue, the more secure the relationship, and the more independent each person will be! Amazing, isn't it?

I'm not suggesting that you force yourself to stop flirting or sending sexual energy away from the relationship. *Making* yourself do it doesn't bring inside-out monogamy. It only brings the outside-in, rule-based form. Instead, we want to use sexual energy and relationship skills in such a way that we get to *discover monogamy.*

MONOGAMY

Back to monogamy! Here is where lies the beauty of cleaning up the harmful influences on our sexuality. As we perceive the interference caused by flirting, lusting, scanning those around us, porn and fantasy, we can move to the truth of our human instincts. We can discover what it's like to never want sex with someone other than our mate! Where the idea that sex with someone new would be more stimulating and exciting is so absurd that you shake your head in amazement. And at the thought that a "sexy" body would be sexually stimulating and bring a kind of pleasure that your aging mate would not. When you know that sexualized attention isn't really attention—it doesn't mean anything about you, it just means that the other person wants attention from you.

Sex based on a melting together that brings monogamy is the kind that makes it easier to co-create your lives together—to solve problems, heal conflicts, and avoid distancing. And then, in an upward spiral, the ease of relating out of bed brings an even deeper possibility when sexual. And around and around. Instead of typical circular arguments you can have circular love making.

In the beginning you may have to trust that this is possible, and take the known paths to work toward it. New love is a great asset in this endeavor, as there is usually more passion and perception of each other as wonderful than after the flaws appear, as well as the conflicts and methods of solving them.

LOVE WITHOUT MONOGAMY?

Many partners of sex addicts ask if it is possible for their partner to love them if they are having affairs or other sexual behavior that is outside of the marriage. Yes, it is.

I see monogamy as a continuum from the absence of it to the completely safe, relationship-enhancing form I have described. Somewhere in the middle, sexual bonding can occur while one partner uses that sexual bonding energy to attach to others, too. One client learned that her husband had been having affairs for 35 years. She was devastated, of course. As she took time to heal from this deep betrayal, she worried over the possibility that her husband had never loved her. How could he love other women, too?

If monogamous love is on a continuum, it is possible that he loved her *and* other women. Sadly, he was deprived of the experience of pouring all of his love into one relationship. But it doesn't mean that he didn't feel affection and love, and take pleasure in sharing his life with her. They had children together, shared homes and bed, and engaged in activities, all of which are bonding. The "love" he felt for other women was based on his need for intense attention. He wanted that strong eye contact that comes with sexual attraction. He didn't want to leave his wife for anyone else, he just wanted something more.

While this man was not at all monogamous, he wasn't at the end of the continuum experienced by those who do not use sex to attach at all. Some people who marry can engage in sex with partners or others in such a way that attachment does not occur. Sex based on lusting, "body parting," and "getting off" is kept separate from the kind of falling in love we are programmed for.

WORKING TOGETHER TO HEAL UNHEALTHY SEXUALITY

If you can see that almost no one has a full use of sexuality to attach to their mate, then you can pay attention to how sex serves you and how it doesn't. Then, when you find someone of interest, you can get to work with your new partner on honing this essential component of love relationships. Instead of increasing arousal with outside-in stimulation, such as sexual fantasy and even pornography, you can elect to focus entirely on each other. This may very well bring up discomfort because of sexual shame and the requirements of being "good in bed." Together, you can examine each rule that intrudes so you can release the shame. As you join together to invite arousal to come only from love, you open yourselves to the most powerful, loving, attaching glue. But it won't happen by itself.

Couples often find that sex goes well in the beginning because they have strong feelings of love, and because they are temporarily blinded to each other's faults. Then, *as conflicts surface and faults are visible, sex can fall into the arena of irresolvable issues.* Since people typically have difficulty talking about sex, it is even more difficult to address than the issues of money, children, religion and families.

First, take a look at all those social rules that interfere with loving. Things like: once you get started you can't stop, you are obligated to continue until orgasm. Orgasms are the definition of the end of "having sex." Men are required to be always ready, have an erection on demand, and perform. Women are suppose to look a certain way.

Then there is the question of how to get started. If one person "initiates," and the other "responds," the difficulty of deciding when to do either without talking about it comes up. A truly united couple won't have this issue because they will both want sex or both not want it. But in the beginning, neither of you will be able to access this knowing well.

Once the initial mutual desire wears off, then come the conflicts over frequency. Particularly deadly is the idea that men and women have differing physiological needs. Some experts try to explain the differences by saying that it is biologically how we are. However, it is just as easy to make up why this isn't true at all, given that for procreation, both genders needn't have sex very often.

If the second purpose of sex is to bond a couple, then it makes sense that an Attached couple will want sex when it is needed for bonding, and not need it when the attachment feels secure. We differ based on gender when sex is a lust-driven, physiological release—and when it is used as a substitute for the deeper, broader expression of love and attachment.

You can discover sexual relating
in which you both want
the same sexual frequency!

When learning your way into how to use sex for its glue purpose, attending to all arenas of relating at the same time can be optimal. Working with your Attachment styles, changing styles of resolving conflict, and healing your unhealthy individual and couple sexuality can all interact to provide a sexual relationship that evolves naturally as part of your life, and part of your coupling.

Chapter 18

Those Who Cannot Be in Relationship

I'm sorry to say there are people who are just not cut out for deeply intimate, healthy relationships. It is possible for almost anyone to engage in extensive individual and group therapy in order to become capable, but many people will have to adjust to a life with only friends and acquaintances.

Those of you who want to believe that the person you find interesting is capable of entering a Securely Attached relationship need to assess if this is actually true. Here are some ideas about how.

People who are psychopathic, extremely narcissistic, or still abusing drugs and alcohol are not available for intimate relating. They will likely be manipulative, controlling, angry, deceitful, and passive aggressive. They land at the far end of Avoidant. They are attached to their substance or process, or to Avoidant maneuvers to keep people away. Even if she is highly social, and has lots of "friends," the level of real attachment with a mate is small.

It can be confusing when these Avoidant people express sadness, remorse, and and are apologetic for their behaviors, especially when they are very enjoyable to be around. I have often heard the sentence, "But he can be so nice [fun, loving]."

Who's Pulling Your Strings, by Harriet Braiker, can help you understand the kind of manipulation and control that is conscious, and that which is not. The person who doesn't know he is manipulating has a difficult time understanding how he causes relationship difficulties. Instead, he thinks the other person is being unreasonable, over-sensitive, making things up, or manipulating. The woman or man who is married to such a person feels crazy. Not only is their reality not validated, they are told that they are having inappropriate reactions. When accusers believe what they say, it can seem impossible to refute. But if you accept what they tell you as true, you cannot help but feel crazy—because it is, in fact, not true!

Partners can become brainwashed into believing they are wrong. Then they either remain in the emotionally chaotic relationship or they leave.

Best to avoid this situation when you are in a position to do so. This is one reason to move very slowly when getting involved. Find out what this person does over a period of time. Discover if you can trust him or not. If any physically or emotionally abusive behaviors appear, do not take the blame – even if you have done something harmful yourself. You may be hurtful, but if you are attacked for it, you will know that this isn't where you should be.

"Nice guys" can be dangerous, too. When they sacrifice in order to be what they think you want, they will want to make you pay for it. Reading *Living with a Passive Aggressive Man*, by Scott Wetzler (even if your date is a woman) will explain this connection. Self-caring people will not want to sacrifice their own needs for someone else. They will eventually resent it, perhaps not know they do, and institute pay-back that makes no sense to the one being paid back.

I have seen active addicts who controlled their partners. One man followed a list of rules his wife gave him, which included not drinking and going to A.A. But he didn't do the 12 steps, did not engage in his psychotherapy sessions, and suppressed his rage over not being allowed to "be himself." He controlled her by "logically" explaining what was wrong with her. It took his wife months to realize that she couldn't change him, and that he wasn't motivated to learn and heal. Then she knew that she had to leave. She couldn't live with his perpetual blame and defensiveness.

If strong Avoidant Attachers are
actively working on these issues, and
can take a look when they appear,
they may become good partners.

The extreme Anxious Attacher has difficulties in relationships, too. The neediness is far greater than normal protest behaviors that emerge when a relationship is threatened. No matter how the partner tries to reassure, it isn't possible to put to rest the fears of abandonment and loss. These needy people may vacillate between the Anxious approach and the Avoidant approach. First they cling, cry, and desire their partner.

But then they pull away, criticize, and emotionally abuse him. When he responds by pulling back, she comes forward again, terrified of loss.

Trying to figure out how to relate with such extremes can be impossible, and best avoided.

Remember how Gottman said that people who use one of the four harmful styles of conflict resolution, and cannot shift to the healthy version, are very likely to divorce? If you're dating someone who uses these styles to the exclusion of healthy ones, this is not a good indicator. Of course you may need to date a while to observe this.

WHEN YOU CANNOT RELATE WELL

What if you are one of those people who depend on defensiveness or other harmful ways of resolving conflict? What if you are way down the continuum of Avoidant Attachment? Do you tend to think the other person is always at fault? Are you unable to see how you may be triggering his responses? Is it all a mystery? Do you just want her to be calm, loving, affectionate, and not confrontive?

•Alex lives alone, has one good friend who lives nearby, and acquaintances developed over time. Once divorced, he realized that this was a preferable way to live. He has many e-mail buddies collected over the years from various jobs and activities. He engages in on-line sexual chat for the romantic connection that he wants to keep separate from his actual life. He has many solitary activities that he enjoys. Alex is not unhappy.

•Rich lives alone, has many solitary activities, reads a lot, works out, and takes care of his home. He differs from Alex in that he usually has a woman in his life to spend time with and has sex. He thinks about the woman when he is home alone. He prefers this to living together and marrying.

•Alice lives alone, puts a lot of energy into her home, created her own successful business, and has two dogs she dearly loves. Her work exposes her to many people, and includes business lunches, dinners and events. She has a social life without closeness. She would date someone for a while, but was soon disappointed. One man was Avoidant, too, and gave his cat more affection than he gave Alice. After resenting this, she realized that being alone worked well.

These people have made valid life choices. They are either not interested in or unwilling to take on the challenge of healing their Attachment style, their histories, or their method of resolving conflicts. They will likely spend their lives engaging in this manner.

WHEN YOU WANT CHANGE

If you want to be able to have a good relationship, then you can take on the task of healing. This involves working with a therapist who is trained in attachment deprivation and abuse. Group therapy provides a number of people giving you information about how you push others away, as well as how you invite closeness. Being with others who are doing the same reduces shame, and is educational, too. If you are using substances or activities in order to avoid, you will need to address this. Giving up alcohol and drugs, and the addictive use of food, sex, etc. will open up those emotions that can heal past deprivation and abuse. It can be difficult, but for those who take it on, it is rewarding.

Chapter 19

THE FIRST DATE – TRANSPARENCY WITH BOUNDARIES

Have you read the many articles about what to do and not do on a first date? About how to select the right person? How to convince him that you are a good candidate? How to guarantee a second date? How to get any man to fall in love with you?

In other words,
how to manipulate and control?

TRANSPARENCY

The route to a Securely Attached relationship is quite the opposite.

*Revealing who you are, what you are feeling in the moment,
and whatever you think, offers the other person
a true glimpse of you.*

If your date doesn't want to do the same, then he or she may not be open to a Secure Attachment.

Being your transparent self doesn't mean revealing everything, however. This person is a stranger. You don't know what she will do with what you reveal. It takes time to trust someone enough to reveal very personal information.

BOUNDARIES

How do you tell the difference between valuable revealing and appropriate boundaries?

This question has no easy answer, but perhaps has some loose guidelines. You might go over the components of secure relationships. Your date's reactions will give you information about her interest in these facets of relating. If none of it makes sense, then you know that you will move on. While this person could potentially be of interest, she probably won't join you in these security-creating approaches. How good to learn this right away and not put in time and effort, or, worse, *attach*, only to discover that it isn't going to work out.

BOUNDARIED TRANSPARENCY

The word "honesty" is frequently misinterpreted. "Transparency" can be, too. Revealing who you are, and what you think and feel, doesn't mean telling your secrets, answering all questions, and providing your entire history.

Healthy relationships include revealing your past, how you operate in various situations, details of growing up, past relationships, and sexual preferences, to name only a few. But this information flows out gradually as you discover that you want to be together. Back and forth, back and forth, trust develops as you each reveal. Then you want to reveal more. But on that first date you are with a stranger. Revealing what you are feeling right there in his presence can be a great opening to a relationship, but you don't know where this is going. The degree of openness that is most powerful – assuming that you find this person interesting enough for a second date – comes from letting yourself be seen.

BEFORE THE DATE

Let's start with the plan for the date. Are you nervous? Most people feel some discomfort over this new event with the potential for connection or rejection. Instead of trying to hide the nervousness, how about saying it right out? "I'm looking forward to meeting you, and I have to say, I'm nervous!" Something like that?

I am sometimes nervous before important professional meetings. I learned that if I take the freedom to name what I feel, I no longer feel it! There is something about having to look right, or do it right, that brings on that nervousness. But if I get to just be myself, then it no longer matters how others respond. So they like me or they don't. But if I set out to create an impression—in other words, manipulate their perception of me—then shame from thinking I should hide myself interferes!

Some of the suggestions in dating articles can be useful, such as asking questions to invite opening up, especially if your date appears nervous. Some people deal with their awkwardness by talking about themselves, or worse, politics, and don't express interest in the other person's thoughts. Then decisions about meeting again are not based on who these two people really are.

Questions about what each wants in a relationship are appropriate during e-mail communication and phone conversations. No need to wait for that first date. I have offered a few possibilities below.

QUESTIONS TO CONSIDER

1. Have you read *Create New Love*? It's about Securely Attached relationships and what to do to get them to grow more easily than usual dating does.

2. I read that asking questions can make things go more easily, so I would like to ask you some questions. What do you think? Or do you want to ask me some?

3. I'd really like to get to know you, who you are, and I'm not sure how to go about that. Have any ideas?

4. What about kissing? I never know on a first date if that's the right thing to do. I'd rather wait even if we want to meet again, especially if we want to meet again, but I didn't want you to think that I'm not interested if I don't kiss you. Or worse, if I don't respond if you start to kiss me!

5. Yikes, my heart rate is going up. I'm sure my blood pressure is too. This would be so much easier if we had known each other as friends. Or would it? Changing from casual to a date always makes me

feel something different. What if we don't like each other? Or one of us likes the other and the other doesn't?

6. I've been married two times, but I have some discomfort telling you in case you would judge me. But really, I do need to know if that makes a difference to you. Please tell me the truth.

If these statements seem too forward, let your facial expressions communicate. Smile when you feel like it; reveal embarrassment if it comes; show interest; smile with pleasure.

CONCLUSION

Well, here we are at the end of the book. As you can see, all these pages are truly a summary of information from many sources. If you choose to look at different approaches to relationships, I recommend that you read the books I listed in the introduction. Relationships are complex, and the experts have accessed a great deal of new information about their nature and nurturing.

The belief that we aren't two independent people who live together and have sex while basically remaining separate has been disproved by studies of not only hormone connections between lovers, but also by actual changes in the brain. Attachment Theory has shown us so much that has gone against some of the logical approaches of mental health.

We know that we have to honor this connection between two people. We have to learn how to create it, take care of it, nurture it, and repair it. Because we live in a shame-driven world, most of us have had difficulty remembering how. Connecting is, however, embedded in our instincts, and we can discover how to re-access all of our knowing of the best attachment.

Now we understand that pain appearing in relationships is most likely the result of one or both members *not knowing how to take care of each other*. And we know many ways of discovering exactly how to. You can learn!

So let's learn together.

THE END

ACKNOWLEDGEMENTS

I would like to thank Katherine Hamilton, Alan Zimmerman, Jim Colborn, Dave Agner, and Kristina Gray for reading the entire manuscript and giving valuable feedback. Danielle, Martha and Mark offered ongoing support and critique in our writers' group. Merry Nell Colborn and Craig Fullmer flooded me with love, questions, and support as I worked my way through this project. I love you guys! The women's Meetup group became a group-united as we studied these principles together, and the men's group hashed out the subject of men's shame. Etsel Skelton offered his expertise in a supportive, educational way.

Thank you all.

ABOUT THE AUTHOR

Anne Stirling Hastings, Ph.D. received her doctorate in psychology from the California School of Professional Psychology and has been in practice in California, Alaska, Washington State and Hawaii. She has specialized in sexuality for 25 years, and is the author of five self-help books and one for professionals. Over the course of helping people with sexuality, she came to see the need to pay attention to the role of shame. Now she is integrating her own studies with those of others to create a practice for people who want to prepare for the best, most loving lives—and relationships. She lives in the Greater Los Angeles area.

Appendix A:

QUESTIONS REGARDING ATTACHMENT PROJECTIONS

1. How did your mother express love when you were a baby? A toddler? An older child? An adult?
2. How were you disciplined at each of those ages?
3. How did your father express love at those stages?
4. How did your father discipline at those stages?
5. How did your parents express love toward each other?
6. How did they express displeasure with each other?
7. Were you separated from your mother before age five? Such as through hospitalizations, birth of siblings, severe illness, etc.
8. Were you attached to other people?
9. What were your first dates like? What was your age during each? How many were there? What was the level of sexual activity?
10. How dependent did you feel in each of these?
11. What was your first extended relationship like? Your first marriage or live-together relationship? Any subsequent marriages or live-together relationships?
12. How dependent did you feel in each of these?
13. What role did sexuality play in each casual and serious relationships? Did it "glue" you together?
14. What was the ending of each relationship like? Easy? Relief? Painful? Devastating?
15. How do you feel about your next relationship: hopeful, hopeless, cautious, concerned, suspicious, angry, etc.?

See the workbook on CreateNewLove.com for more exercises.

16006252R00078

Made in the USA
Charleston, SC
30 November 2012